CHRISTIAN
DISCIPLINES

CHRISTIAN DISCIPLINES

OSWALD CHAMBERS

Discovery House
PUBLISHERS

BOX 3566 • GRAND RAPIDS, MI 49501

*PUBLISHING BOOKS THAT FEED
THE SOUL WITH THE WORD OF GOD.*

Christian Disciplines
Copyright ©1936 by Oswald Chambers Publications Association

This edition copyright ©1995 by Oswald Chambers Publications
Association Limited

Discovery House Publishers is affiliated with RBC Ministries,
Grand Rapids, Michigan 49512

Discovery House books are distributed to the trade by
Thomas Nelson Publishers, Nashville, Tennessee 37214

Library of Congress Cataloging-in-Publication Data

Chambers, Oswald, 1874–1917.
Christian disciplines / Oswald Chambers.
p.   cm.
Previously published in 1985 in 2 separate volumes by
Zondervan Publishing House, Grand Rapids, Michigan

ISBN: 0–929239–64–4

1. Christian life. I. Title.
BV4501.C354   1995
248.4—dc20   94–30010
CIP

Printed in the United States of America

95 96 97 98 99/ CHG / 10 9 8 7 6 5 4 3 2

CONTENTS

The Discipline of Divine Guidance 9

The Discipline of Suffering 45

The Discipline of Peril 79

The Discipline of Prayer 111

The Discipline of Loneliness 151

The Discipline of Patience 201

Publisher's Foreword

We live in an age of "free spirits" and individualism where instant gratification is a trademark and a disciplined lifestyle is dismissed as being out of date, demanding, and unnecessary—a regimen reserved for those who are uneducated and unenlightened. Yet even the most free spirited among us have to face the reality of hardship, pain, and suffering. Sooner or later this side of life gets us and we are forced to ask "Why?" and "What purpose does this serve?"

Oswald Chambers said that "the reason we are all being disciplined is so that we will know that God is real." A profound answer.

At the beginning of the twenty-first century, we believe serious Christians need a new introduction to the disciplines God uses to shape us, expressed in the words of Oswald Chambers, one of the most profound Bible teachers of the twentieth century. We need to understand God's purpose in allowing suffering and hardship, in permitting loneliness and testing, in requiring prayer and patience, and in providing guidance when our path seems treacherous and uncharted. Such disciplines are God's way of molding us, of capturing our attention so that we focus on Him and not on ourselves. They are His means for us to know Him.

These studies were originally given as lectures and later written and published in individual pamphlets by Mrs. Biddy Chambers between the years 1934 and 1938. They were compiled and published in two volumes in 1973 and are now released in a newly-edited one-volume edition for a new generation of Oswald Chambers readers.

The Publisher

1

The Discipline of Divine Guidance

God is not a supernatural interferer; God is the everlasting portion of His people. When a person "born from above" begins his new life he meets God at every turn, hears Him in every sound, sleeps at His feet, and wakes to find Him there. He is a new creature in a new creation, with tribulation developing his power of knowing God, till on some transfiguration morning, he finds himself entirely sanctified by God; and from that unspeakable bliss God loosens him from heaven, a "pilgrim of eternity," to do a work for Him among men. Out he goes, a person any may take advantage of, but none dare. His childlike simplicity excites the ridicule of society, but a wall of fire encircles him. His ignorance of the way he takes makes the cunning of the age laugh at the ease with which they think they can utilize him for their own ends. But lo! they are caught in their own snare, and their wisdom is turned to sorrow and foolishness. Such a person becomes a spectacle to angels and to other people. Nothing can daunt him, nothing frighten him, nothing deflect him. He may be tried by cruel mockings and scourgings, by bonds and imprisonment. He may be stoned or sawn in two, tempted or slain with the sword. He may wander about in sheepskins and goatskins. He may be destitute, afflicted, tormented. He may home in deserts, and mountains, in dens and caves of the earth. But ever, by some mysterious mystic touch, we know he is one "of whom the world was not worthy" (Hebrews 11:38). All heaven and earth and hell are "persuaded that neither death nor life, nor angels nor principalities nor powers, nor things present nor things to come, nor height nor depth, nor any other created thing, shall be able to separate us from the love of God which is in Christ Jesus our Lord" (Romans 8:38–39).

The child's mind is the only mind to which God can appeal, and our Lord went deeper than the most profound philosophy in the incident recorded in Mark 9:36–37: "Then He took a little child and set him in the midst of them. And when He had taken him in His arms, He said to them, 'Whoever receives one of these little children in My name receives Me; and whoever receives Me, receives not Me but Him who sent Me.' " As soon as the gates of the head are closed on our experiences we limit God, and by sealing our minds we limit our growth and the possibility of graduating in divine guidance. The child's heart is open to any and all avenues; an angel would no more surprise it than a person. In dreams, in visions, in visible and invisible ways, God can talk and reveal Himself to a child; but this profound yet simple way is lost forever as soon as we lose the open, childlike nature.

By every standard we know except one, the God of the Bible is a confusing contradiction to Himself. The God who caused to be written: "You shall not murder," commanded Abraham to offer "your only son Isaac, whom you love, . . .

as a burnt offering" (Genesis 22:2). The God who said: "You shall not commit adultery," commanded His servant Hosea to marry a harlot (Hosea 1:2). Jesus Christ Himself presents a similar dilemma to every standard, except one. He tells the seventy: "Behold, I give you the authority to trample on serpents and scorpions, and over all the power of the enemy, and nothing shall by any means hurt you" (Luke 10:19). Again He tells His disciples: "They will put you out of the synagogues; yes, the time is coming that whoever kills you will think that he offers God service" (John 16:2). And the apostle Paul, who said he had "the mind of Christ," wrote to the Corinthians: "Why do you not rather accept wrong? Why do you not rather let yourselves to be cheated?" (1 Corinthians 6:7); and yet when being tried himself, he said, "I appeal to Caesar" (Acts 25:11).

God Himself, our Lord Jesus Christ, and the saints are examples of contradiction judged by every standard except one, namely, the standard of personal responsibility to God on the basis of personal character.

In testing circumstances saints decide differently—may all the different decisions be correct? Unquestionably they may, for the decisions are made on the basis of personal character in its responsibility to God. The blunder of the saint lies in saying, "Because I decide thus in this crisis, therefore that is the rule for all." Nonsense! God is sovereign and His ways are discernible according to the attainment of the particular character. One of the most fallacious lines of reasoning is on the line of a hypothesis in the matter of God's will. No saint knows what he will do in circumstances he has never been in. "I want you to be without care" (1 Corinthians 7:32), says the apostle Paul. A saint is a creature of vast possibilities knit into shape by the ruling personality of God.

Supernatural voices, dreams, ecstasies, visions, and manifestations, may or may not be an indication of the will of God. The words of Scripture, the advice of the saints, strong impressions during prayer, may or may not be an indication of the will of God. The one test given in the Bible is discernment of a personal God and personal relationship with Him, witnessed to ever after in walk and conversation. A striking line of demarcation discernible between the guidance of God and all other guidance is that all other supernatural guidance loses sight of human personality and of divine personality, and ends in a swoon into absolute nothingness. In every stage of divine guidance which the Bible records, these two elements become ever clearer: God and myself. The most intense statement of this is made by our Lord:

"Jesus answered him, 'The first of all the commandments is: "Hear, O Israel: The LORD our God, the LORD is one. And you shall love the LORD your God with all your heart, with all your soul, with all your mind, and with all your strength" . . . . And the second, like it, is this: "You shall love your neighbor as yourself." There is no other commandment greater than these' " (Mark 12:29–31).

The eternal truth is that God created me to be distinctly not Himself, but to realize Him in perfect love. If I allow that God teaches me to walk in His will, I shall allow my neighbor, whom I love as myself, the same certainty, although his way may seem so different. "What is that to you? You follow Me."

Professor W. James in *The Varieties of Religious Experiences,* says:

Among the visions and messages some have always been too patently silly; among the trances and convulsive seizures some have been too fruitless for conduct and character, to pass themselves off as significant, still less as divine. In the history of Christian mysticism the problem how to discriminate between such messages and experiences as were really divine miracles, and such others as the demon in his malice was able to counterfeit, thus making the religious person twofold more the child of hell than he was before, has always been a difficult one to solve, needing all the sagacity and experience of the best directors of conscience. In the end it had to come to our Imperialist Criterion. "By their fruits you will know them," not by their roots. Jonathan Edwards' *Treatise on Religious Affections,* is an elaborate working out of this thesis. The roots of a man's virtue are inaccessible to us. No appearances whatever are infallible proofs of grace. Our practice is the only sure evidence, even to ourselves, that we are genuine Christians.

When all religions and philosophies and philologies have tried to define God, one and all sink inane and pass, while the Bible's statements stand like eternal monuments, shrouded in ineffable glory: "God is light"; "God is love"; "God is holy." Every attempted definition of God other than these sublime inspirations negates God, and we find ourselves possessed of our own ideas with never a glimpse of the living God. When the flatteries, eulogies, enthusiasms and extravagances regarding Jesus Christ have become enshrined sentiments in poetry, music and eloquence, they pass, like fleeting things of mist, colored but for a moment by reflected splendors from the Son of God. And our Lord's own words come with the sublime staying of the simple gentleness of God: "I am the way, the truth, and the life."

When art has fixed her ideals, and contemplation has cloistered her choicest souls, and devotion has traced her tremulous records, quivering with the unbearable pathos of martyrdom, we realize that all these miss the portrayal of the saint. And again the severe adequacy of Scripture, undeflected by earth's heartbreaks, or griefs, or sorrows, remains the true portrait of the saint: saved, sanctified, and sent.

It is when silenced by such considerations as these that we can behold the child-heart nestling in the arms of God, playing about the path of the Lord Jesus Christ, or hasting with willing feet to souls perishing in the wilderness. It is only thus, with chastened, disciplined, stilled hearts that we whisper out before His throne, "I have heard of You by the hearing of the ear, but now my eye sees You. Therefore I abhor myself, and repent in dust and ashes" (Job 42:5-6).

"Then Moses said to the Lord, 'See, You say to me, "Bring up this people." But You have not let me know whom You will send with me. Yet You have said, "I know you by name, and you have also found grace in My sight." Now therefore, I pray, if I have found grace in Your sight, show me now Your way, that I may know You and that I may find grace in Your sight. And consider that this nation is Your people.' And He said, 'My Presence will go with you, and I will give you rest' " (Exodus 33:12-14).

> Little lamb, who made thee?
> Dost thou know who made thee,
> Gave thee life, and bid thee feed
> By the stream and o'er the mead,
> Gave thee clothing of delight,
> Softest clothing, woolly, bright,
> Gave thee such a tender voice,
> Making all the vales rejoice?

Little lamb, who made thee?
Dost thou know who made thee?

Little lamb, I'll tell thee:
Little lamb, I'll tell thee:
He is called by thy name,
For He calls Himself a Lamb,
He is meek, and He is mild,
He became a little child.
I a child, and thou a lamb,
We are called by His name.
Little lamb, God bless thee!
Little lamb, God bless thee!

By God's Sayings
(First Stage)

How often in the Bible we read such words as those in Genesis 12:1: "Now the LORD said to Abram," and in Ezekiel 1:3: "The word of the LORD came expressly to Ezekiel," and in Matthew 7:24: "Whoever hears these sayings of Mine, and does them, I will liken him to a wise man, who built his house on the rock."

What is the Word of God? Where are the sayings of God? The answer is readily given: "The Bible is the Word of God." But we must ask again, because we have all known battlers for the Bible as the Word of God whom we should hesitate to call saints, for many have proved logically what never came to pass from the Bible. Consequently the answer is given more cautiously: "The Bible contains the Word of God." This is a most ingenious fallacy and leads to a mystical type of religious life which by being "special," speedily becomes spurious (see 2 Peter 1:20).

The Bible is the Word of God only to those who are born from above and who walk in the light. Our Lord Jesus Christ—the Word of God, and the Bible—the *words* of God, stand or fall together, they can never be separated without fatal results. A man's attitude to our Lord determines his attitude to the Bible. The "sayings" of God to a person not born from above are of no consequence; to him the Bible is simply a remarkable compilation of literature. All the confusion arises from not recognizing this. But to the soul born from above, the Bible is the universe of God's revealed will. The Word of God to me is ever according to my spiritual character; it makes clear my responsibility to God as well as my individuality apart from Him.

A quotation from an able article in the *Spectator* as long ago as April 13, 1907, entitled, "The Mind of Christ" will serve well:

> If we refuse to look at the Gospel as a whole and to use our reason; if we insist on making of Christ what He distinctly refused to be, a ruler and a judge, instead of the *Light of the World,* we may set up tyrannies as bad as, or worse than, those instituted by Roman dogmatism. There will be no new Torquemadas, but how much suffering may not be caused by a new Tolstoy. Upon isolated sentences of Jesus absolutely conflicting systems may be erected, and a measure of fanaticism is natural to humanity. . . . But we may not forget that there is an indifference which plumes itself on its moderation, and is even more opposed to the mind of Christ than fanaticism.

What applies to our present dispensation is exactly the same in principle as applied to the hoary antiquity, namely, that the pure in heart see and hear God. The stupendous profundities of God's will, surging with unfathomable mysteries, come down to the shores of common life, not in emotions and fires, nor in aspirations and vows, agonies and visions, but in a way so simple that wayfarers, though fools, cannot make a mistake, that is, in words.

It is recorded in Deuteronomy 32:46–47: "And he [Moses] said to them, 'Set your hearts on all the words which I testify among you this day, which you shall command your children to be careful to observe—all the words of this law. For it is not a futile thing for you, because it is your life, and by this word you shall prolong your days in the land which you cross over the Jordan to possess.' " And our Lord in Mark 4:14 states that "The sower sows the word."

As soon as any soul is born from above, the Bible becomes to him the universe of revelation facts, just as the natural world is the universe of common sense facts. These revelation facts are *words* to our faith, not *things*. The stage of divine guidance by God's sayings is reached when a soul understands that, by the tribulations of the providential life, God's Spirit speaks an understanding of His Word never known before. For any soul to teach what he has not bought by suffering is almost sure to bring tribulation which will either destroy or lead to personal understanding of the word taught. Divine guidance by the Word indicates a profound and personal preparation of heart. God's sayings are sealed to every soul until they are opened by the indwelling Spirit of God. How often the individual soul has to learn by a bitter and, in some sense, an altogether uncalled for experience, that—

He placed thee mid this dance
Of plastic circumstance,

This Present, thou, forsooth, wouldst fain arrest:
Machinery just meant
To give thy soul its bent,
Try thee and turn thee forth, sufficiently impressed.

To search for a word of God to suit one's case is never divine guidance, but guidance by human caprice and inclination. The Holy Spirit who brings to our remembrance what Jesus has said and leads us into all truth, does so to glorify Jesus Christ. Divine guidance by the Word always makes us realize our responsibility to God. In tribulations God brings divine guidance by His Word, and as we go on we begin to understand what our Lord said: "The words that I speak to you are spirit, and they are life" (John 6:63). Every interpretation of the sayings of God that does not reveal this fundamental responsibility to God, and a realization that we are to be for the praise of His glory is a private interpretation, and is severely condemned by God.

> . . . We abide
> Not on this earth; but for a little space
> We pass upon it: and while so we pass,
> God through the dark hath set the Light of Life,
> With witness for Himself, the Word of God,
> To be among us Man, with human heart,
> And human language, thus interpreting
> The One great Will incomprehensible,
> Only so far as we in human life
> Are able to receive it.

How often have our misunderstandings of God's Word proved to us the need for the penetrating word of our Lord: "I still have many things to say to you, but you cannot bear them now" (John 16:12). In our prayings, in our desirings, in our patience, does our knowledge of God enable us to say and really mean, "Speak, LORD, for Your servant hears" (1 Samuel 3:9)? Would we really hear God's Word, or are we not rather in this immediate tribulation waiting for God to persuade us that our own way is right after all? Oh, the bliss of that disciplined child-heart, which when He speaks, says, "Yes, Lord," and simply obeys.

> Pining souls! come nearer Jesus,
>   And oh come not doubting thus,
> But with faith that trusts more bravely
>   His huge tenderness for us.
> If our love were but more simple,
>   We should take Him at His word;
> And our lives would be all sunshine
>   In the sweetness of our Lord.

The school of the "Divine Guidance by God's Sayings" is one of severe discipline. It will mean great heart-searchings, great patience, and great simplicity to be guided in this way.

By God's Symbols
(Second Stage)

"And the LORD went before them by day in a pillar of cloud, to lead the way, and by night in a pillar of fire to give them light, so as to go by day and night. He did not take away the pillar of cloud by day or the pillar of fire by night from before the people" (Exodus 13:21–22).

"When you see the ark of the covenant of the LORD your God, and the priests, the Levites, bearing it, then you shall set out from your place and go after it" (Joshua 3:3).

"A man will be as a hiding place from the wind, and as a cover from the tempest, as rivers of water in a dry place, as the shadow of a great rock in a weary land" (Isaiah 32:2).

"And the Holy Spirit descended in bodily form like a dove upon Him, and a voice came from heaven, which said, You are My beloved Son; in You I am well pleased" (Luke 3:22).

The cloudy pillar, the fiery pillar, the ark, the man, the dove, are all God's symbols. This way of divine guidance by symbols is a deep and blessed one. God does not leave us to the vague, ungraspable intuitions of the mind of some great individual for guidance, or to our own vain imaginings. He has made a world of things other than ourselves, the safe-guard and inspiration of our commonsense reasonings; and He has made a world of spiritual realities the safeguard and inspiration of our discernment. It is on this God-created ingredient in human nature that every great organization, good or bad, is based. The revolt against error on one side is ever apt to enter into error on the other. The revolt, for instance, against Roman Catholicism has developed into an irresponsible individualism which is equally unbiblical.

How often our Lord Jesus Christ emphasizes the guid-ance by symbols: "I AM the door"; "I AM the bread of life"; "I AM the true vine"; "I AM the way." A right understanding of this biblical concept is essential to all Christian thinking. The Bible's order seems to be—the absolute truth; the sym-bolic truth; the false.

All that we see on this earth is symbolic reality, and only as the heart is purged from sin can we see the symbol-ism. That's why when a person is in Christ Jesus he is a new creation and he sees everything in the common world as symbols—invisible realities. (Remember, there are sym-bols of the devil and of the kingdom of evil just as there are symbols of God and of the kingdom of heaven.) How simply and clearly our Lord teaches this: "If your eye is bad, your whole body will be full of darkness. If therefore the light that is in you is darkness, how great is that darkness" (Matthew 6:23). And vice versa: "If therefore your eye is good, your whole body will be full of light" (Matthew 6:22). When Jesus heard His Father speak, "The people who stood by and heard it said that it had thundered" (John 12:29). Again, when Saul of Tarsus was met by Jesus on the way to Damascus and heard His voice, the men that journeyed with him saw only sudden lightening and physical collapse.

> Earth's crammed with heaven,
> And every common bush afire with God;
> But only he who sees, takes off his shoes,—
> The rest sit round it and pluck blackberries,
> And daub their natural faces unaware
> More and more from the first similitude!

One is made to turn with weary exhaustion from the unthinking hand-to-mouth experience of much of the religious literature of the day. To *think* as a Christian is a rare accomplishment, especially as the curious leaven which puts a premium on ignorance works its sluggish way. To speak of Plato to the majority of Christian preachers would be to meet not a consciousness of ignorance, but a blatant pride which boasts of knowing nothing outside the Bible, which, in all probability, means knowing nothing inside it either. Christian thinking is a rare and difficult thing; so many seem unaware that the first great commandment according to our Lord is, "You shall love the LORD your God . . . with all your mind" (Mark 12:30).

No mind, other than the mind of our Lord, has so profoundly expounded this line of guidance by symbols as
Plato. He saw with a clearness of vision second only to
the inspired prophets of God. No wonder many in the
early thoughtful days of Christianity wanted to class him
as Father of the Church. It is impossible for people to be
guided by absolute truth. God, who is absolute truth, said
to Moses: "You cannot see My face; for no man shall see
Me, and live" (Exodus 33:20). God guides us stage by
stage, and the most marvelous stage of His guidance is by
symbols.

What are we to understand by a symbol? A symbol
represents a spiritual truth by means of image or properties
of natural things. A symbol must not be taken as an allegory. An allegory is simply a figurative discourse with a
meaning other than that contained in literal words. A symbol is sealed until the right spirit is given for its understanding and God's symbols are undetected unless His
Spirit is in His child to enable him to understand. What did
the cloudy pillar by day or the fiery pillar by night signify
to the hordes in the desert? Nothing more than the mystery
of ever varying cloud forms. To the children of God they
meant the manifested guidance of God. How a person inter-
prets God's symbols reveals what manner of person he is.
How often we have to say with the psalmist, "I was like a
beast before You" (Psalm 73:22), without understanding.
How often the ass recognizes that one of God's angels is
speaking before the so-called prophet on its back detects it.

> All that meets the bodily sense I deem
> Symbolical—one mighty Alphabet
> For infant minds! And we in this low world
> Placed with our backs to bright Reality,

That we may learn with young, unwounded ken
The Substance from the Shadow!

God shifts His symbols and we know not why; but God is ever only good, and the shifting of one symbol means surely that another symbol is to guide us to a nearer grasp of Himself. When God has left a symbol, it becomes transparent, so to speak, and has no further binding force. How sad it is under the sun to see people worshipping a symbol which has been abandoned by God. How degenerate, how idolatrous, how ensnaring it becomes when God's voice sounds to the spirit of a child of His: "See! Your house is left to you desolate" (Matthew 23:38). We are not to worship reminiscences; this is the characteristic of all other religions, saving the Bible-based religion. The Bible-based religion is one of eternal progress, an intense and militant going on. A perilous time ensues for the individual and for the religious world whenever God shifts His symbols. Obedience to the voice of the Spirit within, the Word of God without, and the suffering of the tribulation around, enable the child of God to hear God's voice and recognize His changing symbols. This discipline of divine guidance by symbols is a serious, momentous discipline and God never leaves His children alone in such times, for,

. . . behind the dim unknown
Standeth God within the shadows,
Keeping watch upon His own.

The worship of a past symbol is not a whit more dangerous than the irresponsible individualism that refuses to have any symbol. Both are contrary to God's Word and God's ways. Where do we stand today with regard to God's great symbols? Is it a selfish isolation, an unholy "come-out-ism?" Then may God hand us the wine cup from the hand of a despised church member until our spiritual dullness is discerned and our spiritual pride humbled. Or is it a dead symbolism, cast aside in the economy of God, a moribund ritualism? If so, may the Spirit sting our traditional "churchianity" into going "outside the camp, bearing His reproach" (Hebrews 13:13).

> Blind me with seeing tears until I see!
> Let not fair poetry, science, art, sweet tones,
> Build up about my soothed sense a world
> That is not Thine, and wall me up in dreams;
> So my sad heart may cease to beat with Thine,
> The great World-heart, whose blood forever shed
> Is human life; whose ache is man's dumb pain.

> As year by year the thrills of springtide shoot
> Through earth's dull veins, with fresh, magnetic might,
> Nor fail, for frosts that nip and winds that blight,
> So, Lord, who erst didst stir with quickening power
> My answering soul, achieve what Thou hast aimed;
> Draw, for Thou hast drawn; hold, what Thou hast
>   claimed.

> Draw through all failure to the perfect Flower;
> Draw through all darkness to the perfect Light.
> Yea, let the rapture of Thy springtide thrill
> Through me, beyond me, till its ardour fill
> The lingering souls that know not Thee aright;
> That Thy great love may make of me, even me,
> One added link to bind the world to Thee.

By God's Servants
(Third Stage)

Indeed I have given him as a witness to the people,
a leader and commander for the people.

(Isaiah 55:4)

Guidance by God's sayings has to bring the soul into the surgery of events before a new listening attitude can be gained to those sayings. At first the soul hears in one direction only, namely, that of its prejudices. Guidance by God's symbols makes it clear to the heart that outward vision is only possible as the inward eye is opened; and as God touches the eye with salve, the soul realizes that the changing symbols give deeper and more penetrating visions of God.

Guidance by His servants gives a yet more intimate nearness to God Himself. It is during this discipline that we learn that no ideal is of any practical avail unless it be incarnated. If the mystic spell of nature in its rolling air, its eternal uplands and abiding plains, its sunrise dawning and setting glories, its perennial springs, and summer nights languishing to autumn, the strenuous grip of its icy colds—if these awaken a sense of the sublime and the unreached, it ends but in a spontaneous ache when the deep within calls to the deep outside.

If the imprisoned soul of sound makes the human spirit weep tears from too deep a well to be reached by individual suffering; if music turns the human heart into a vast capacity for something as yet undreamed of till all its being aches to the verge of infinity; if the minor reaches of our music have awakened harmonies in spheres we know not, till with dumb yearnings we turn our sightless orbs, "crying like children in the night, with no language but a cry"; if painters' pictures stop the ache which nature started and fill for one amazing moment the yearning abysses discovered by the more mysterious thing than joy in music's movements—it is but for a moment. And all seems but to have increased our capacity for a crueler sensitivity, a more useless agony of suffering. But when God's servants guide us to His heart, then the first glorious outlines of the meaning of it all pass before us.

If we trace the lineaments of the servants of God in the Bible, we find a servant of God to be altogether different from an instrument of God. An instrument of God is one whom God takes up and uses and puts down again. A servant of God is one who has given up forever *his right to himself,* and is bound to his Lord as His slave. "For he who is called in the Lord, while a slave is the Lord's freedman. Likewise he who is called while free is Christ's slave" (1 Corinthians 7:22).

An instrument is one who shows God's sovereignty, an unaccountable sovereignty maybe, but unchallengeable ever. A servant is one who, recognizing God's *sovereign* will, leaps to do that will of his own *free choice.*

What shall we say then? Is there unrighteousness with God? Certainly not! For He says to Moses, "I will have mercy on whomever I will have mercy, and I will have compassion on whomever I will have compassion." So then, it is not of him who wills, nor of him who runs, but of God who shows mercy. For the Scripture says to the Pharaoh, "For this very purpose I have raised you up, that I may show My power in you, and that My name may be declared in all the earth." Therefore He has mercy on whom He wills, and whom He wills He hardens.

You will say to me then, "Why does He still find fault? For who has resisted His will?" But indeed, O man, who are you to reply against God? Will the thing formed say to him who formed it, "Why have you made me like this?" Does not the potter have power over the clay, from the same lump to make one vessel for honor and another for dishonor? (Romans 9:14–21)

Guidance by His servants! What a blessed guidance, but oh, it is stern. "A servant of God"—the meaning of this phrase is largely lost today. The phrase that suits our modern mood better is, "a servant of men." Our watch-word today is, "The greatest good for the greatest num-ber." The watchcry of the servant of God is, "The greatest obedience to my Lord." How many of us know a servant of God who has a right understanding of the sci-ence of God and can introduce us to Him, and to His thoughts and His hopes? We are oversatiated with sym-pathizers with people, and with that mystic-sounded shibboleth, "Humanity." To quote G. K. Chesterton, whose insurgent mind is the best cure for any complacent stoicism:

And the same antithesis exists about another modern religion, I mean the religion is as a shadow. The lure the servants of God are made but attracts men to a wilderness wherein God woos men to Himself. Oh, the wild wail of the heart of the man or woman who mistook the fascination of God in His servant for God Himself, and clasped to his or her heart *a man of like passions as we are*! Oh for that man of God who will hand over to God the hearts

God has called through him! It is not *you* who awakened that mighty desire in the heart; it is not *you* who called forth that longing in the spirit; it is God in you. Are you a servant of God? Then point them to Him. Down on your face, down in the dust, oh man of God, if those arms clasp you, and that heart rests on you! If that longing, loving heart awakens and finds you instead of God, what a passion of despair will blight you with the curse of solitariness and silence!

Oh, there are sad cries all over the spiritual world entering into the heart of God, and He will avenge them. Oh that we could hear it—"You have taken the East from me; you have taken the West from me; you have taken what is before me; and what is behind me; you have taken the moon, you have taken the sun from me, and my fear is great, you have taken God from me."

Are all servants of God like that? No, thank God! The sheep are many and the shepherds are few, for the fatigue is staggering, the heights are giddy, and the sights are awful. It is no wonder our Lord said, "The sheep follow him, for they know his voice. Yet they will by no means follow a stranger, but will flee from him, for they do not know the voice of strangers" (John 10:4–5).

One of the greatest of these servants of God said he was a voice that cried but one thing: "Repent"; that pointed in but one direction: "Behold the Lamb of God!" That is what a servant of God is for. Aye, and what a school God puts His servant through! Its years of graduation are—Separation, Sorrow, Supreme Sanctification and Suffering.

Is there one man in disenchanted days
Who yet has feet on earth and head in Heaven?
One viceroy yet to whom his King hath given
The fire that kindles and the strength that sways?
Is there a wisdom whose extremest ways
Lead upward still? For us who most have striven,
Made wise too early and too late forgiven,
Our prudence palsies and our seeing slays.
We are dying; is there one alive and whole,
A hammer of the Lord, a simple soul,
Man with the men and with the boys a boy?
We are barren, let a male and conquering voice
Fill us and quicken us and make rejoice,
Even us who have so long forgotten joy.

God guides by His servants, and it is a guidance that disciplines heart and mind and spirit. Watch this guidance through the records of Holy Writ about the careers of Abraham, Moses, Joshua, Gideon, and Deborah. Trace the loneliness of their apprenticeship and mastership. Grasp the loneliness of Abraham, "the friend of God." Enter into and imagine the rugged discipline of Moses, who esteemed "the reproach of Christ greater riches than the treasures in Egypt" (Hebrews 11:26). Bow before the winnowing of the unworldly heart of Joshua. Marvel as you see how God took timid Gideon as His wardrobe, and clothed Himself with him. And be silent before Deborah, that sibyl of God's sanctity, as she led God's army. And marking their self-effacement and otherworldliness, bow your face before God and learn the strangeness of His guidance by His servants.

Scarcely have we paid enough attention to the prefiguring of our Lord in the prophets and servants of God, and perhaps we have overemphasized His prefiguring in signs and symbols of the dispensations surrounding those prophets and servants. How strangely the writers of the Psalms launch out into a definite prefiguring of our Lord! How wonderfully the sorrows of these servants of God take on new meaning when we see Jesus! The anthropomorphism of the Old Testament can never be dispatched by the statement that it is humanity trying to state God in terms of his own ignorance. It is rather God prefiguring the stupendous mystery of the Incarnation.

> Tis the weakness in strength, that I cry for!
> my flesh, that I seek
> In the Godhead! I seek and find it. O Saul, it
> shall be
> A Face like my face that receives thee;
> a Man like to me,
> Thou shalt love and be loved by, forever:
> a Hand like this hand
> Shall throw open the gates of new life to you!
> See the Christ stand!

By God's Sympathy
(Fourth Stage)

I will mention the lovingkindnesses of the Lord and the praises of the Lord, according to all that the Lord has bestowed on us, and the great goodness toward the house of Israel, which He has bestowed on them according to His mercies, according to the multitude of His lovingkindnesses. For He said, "Surely they are My people, children who will not lie." So He became their Savior. In all their affliction He was afflicted, and the Angel of His Presence saved them; in His love and in His pity He redeemed them; and He bore them and carried them all the days of old (Isaiah 63:7–9).

He found him in a desert land and in the wasteland, a howling wilderness; He encircled him, He
instructed him, He kept him as the apple of His eye.
As an eagle stirs up its nest, hovers over its young,
spreading out its wings, taking them up, carrying
them on its wings, so the LORD alone lead him, and
there was no foreign god with him. (Deuteronomy
32:10–12)

You have also given me the shield of Your salvation; Your right hand has held me up, Your gentleness has made me great. You enlarged my path under
me, so my feet did not slip. (Psalm 18:35–36)

The Sympathy of God

God having feeling for us! The very heart of the phrase
is given in Hebrews 4:15–16, "For we do not have a High
Priest who cannot sympathize with our weaknesses, but
was in all points tempted as we are, yet without sin. Let us
therefore come boldly to the throne of grace, that we may
obtain mercy and find grace to help in time of need."

It is in the mystic tenderness of the guidance by His
sympathy that God gives a love like His own. Oh, how can
language put it when the soul, the individual soul, knows
God has marked all sorrows and has kept all tears till not
one drop is lost, knows that "He knows our frame; He
remembers that we are dust" (Psalm 103:14)? When the first
great surprise of the light of His sympathy bursts the tear-
dimmed soul and turns it into radiant rainbows of promise?
When no *sayings* of His resound on our ears with thrilling
clarion call? When no visible *symbol* disciplines our faltering
steps? When no *servant* of God is near to help us discern
His will? When the cloud gathers round us, and we fear as

we enter the cloud, and Lo! a mystic touch is on our spirits, a coolness and balm, "as one whom his mother comforts" (Isaiah 66:13), so the Lord comforts us? Oh, the tenderest touch of a mother's love is nothing compared to our blessed Father's sympathy! It is there, couched in His arms, that we are guided into that secret of secrets, that it is not men's sins we have to deal with, but their suffering. It is ensphered in the nights when He gives us the treasures of darkness that discipline us to be staying powers in the alarm moments of other lives.

What an atmosphere there breathes about the life God is guiding by His sympathy! We feel a larger horizon, an expanding heart and brain and spirit grasping us and uplifting us. Nothing seems changed, yet a kiss, as if the kiss of God, touches our care, and we smilingly wonder how things have altered, and life is never the same again. From guidance by His sympathy, we learn that God heeds not our faults nor our mistakes; He looks at our hearts. This point, so blessed, so rare, perhaps we could never see before. How gladly, how nobly, how purely we grow under the guidance by God's sympathy!

And yet it would be dangerous if God guided us by His sympathy too soon. Look again at Isaiah 63 for the sad sequel to such guidance: "But they rebelled and grieved His Holy Spirit; so He turned Himself against them as an enemy, and He fought against them" (verse 10). And look again at the sequel in Deuteronomy 32: "But Jeshurun grew fat, and kicked; . . . then he forsook God who made him, and scornfully esteemed the Rock of his salvation" (verse 15).

Clearly, sympathy may be dangerous in its effects on people. In undisciplined, self-centered lives it seems to engender a self-confident vanity that abuses the end and meaning of God's sympathy; the goodness of God, which ought to lead to repentance, leads rather to blatant presumption. But to a nature disciplined and chastened by self-knowledge, whose cynicism (which ever arises from the narrow view of personal limitations) has long since given way to larger, more generous, more self-effacing views—to such a nature, guidance by God's sympathy is an unspeakable boon, ever leading the soul out into deep adoration of God and devotion to Him.

This aspect of guidance by God's sympathy is rarely spoken of by expounders of God's ways with men. This is partly because of the definite indefinability of the guidance, and partly because so few understand it, or have learned to partake in such guidance by those mystic touches which endear the soul to God and God to that soul beyond all words.

Guidance by sympathy amongst ourselves is often questionable because a person may sympathize out of self-sentiment, which is nothing more than disguised selfishness and has an enervating, unennobling effect. Sympathy to benefit and brace and ennoble must spring from a higher source than the one who is suffering has reached as yet. The purpose and heart of our Lord's sympathy is that it does not make one submissive to a broken heart and to degenerate hereditary bondage, but guides to where He will bind up the brokenhearted and set at liberty the captives. There is a distressing snare which besets a certain type of saint—the snare of a morbid desire for sympathy—which simply makes them craving spiritual sponges, so to speak, to mop up sympathy. God's criticism of us, strange to say, does not hurt, for the soul understands that it springs from a deep well of sympathy. Criticism without sympathy is cruel, but criticism that springs from sympathy is blessed.

The discipline of guidance by God's sympathy leads to a clearer, better understanding of God's ideas and hopes and aims. In this way He makes known to us His *ways*; other-wise we simply know His *acts* (see Psalm 103:7). Through guidance by His sympathy we understand that "He doeth all things well," and though He slay, that soul cannot fear. The language of the soul guided by God's sympathy is an amazed rebuke to those who do not know God! For he says by his life, "It is the Lord. Let Him do what seems good to Him."

The guidance by God's sympathy keeps the soul and heart in a rare atmosphere of blessed spiritual love. It is along this line of divine guidance that God takes us into counsel with Himself, as it were, saying as He did about Abraham, "Shall I hide from Abraham what I am doing?" (Genesis 18:17).

Before we take our final meditation and musing on those serene thoughts of guidance by God Himself, let our hearts lie open before that marvel of revelation in the fourteenth chapter of John's gospel, verses 16–18.

"I will pray the Father, and He will give you another Helper, that He may abide with you forever—the Spirit of truth, whom the world cannot receive, because it neither sees Him nor knows him; but you know Him, for He dwells with you and will be in you. I will not leave you orphans; I will come to you."

Call the Helper by the term you think best—Advocate, Comforter, Paraclete, the word conveys the indefinable blessedness of His sympathy—an inward, invisible kingdom that causes the saint to sing through every night of sorrow. This Holy Comforter represents the ineffable motherhood of God. Protestantism has lost for many generations this aspect of the divine revelation because of its violent antipathy to

34   *Christian Disciplines*

Mariolatry as practiced by the Roman Catholic Church; and it behooves us to remember that Protestantism is not the whole gospel of God, but an expression of a view of the gospel of God specially adapted to the crying needs of a particular time.

George MacDonald in his book entitled *Sir Gibbie*, writes as follows (and by the way, it is a striking indication of the trend and shallowness of the modern reading public that George MacDonald's books have been so neglected):

> See revelation culminate in Elizabeth and Mary, the mothers of John the Baptist and Jesus. Think how much fitter that it should be so; that they to whom the Word of God comes should be women bred in the dignity of a natural life, and familiarity with the large ways of the earth; women of simple and few wants, without distraction, and with time for reflection—compelled to reflection, indeed, from the enduring presence of an unsullied consciousness, for wherever there is a humble, thoughtful nature, into that nature the divine consciousness, that is, the Spirit of God, presses as into its own place. Holy women are to be found everywhere, but the prophetess is not so likely to be found in the city as in the hill country.

We quote this simply for the purpose of suggesting how we limit ourselves and our concept of God by ignoring the side of the divine nature best symbolized by womanhood, and the Comforter, be it reverently said, surely represents this side of the divine nature. It is the Comforter who sheds abroad the love of God in our hearts. It is the Comforter who baptizes us into oneness with Jesus, in the amazing language of Scripture, until we are indwelled by a mysterious union with God. It is the Comforter who brings forth the fruit of love, joy, peace, long-suffering, kindness, goodness, faithfulness, meekness, temperance. Guidance by His sympathy leads by a blessed discipline into an understanding of God which passes knowledge.

> . . . that whatsoever spark
> Of pure and true in any human heart
> Flickered and lived, it burned itself towards Him
> In an electric current, through all bonds
> Of intervening race and creed and time,
> And flamed up to a heat of living faith.
> And love, and love's communion, and the joy
> And inspiration of self-sacrifice;
> And drew together in a central coil,
> Magnetic, all the noblest of all hearts,
> And made them one with Him, in a live flame
> That is the purifying and the warmth
> Of all the earth even to these latter days.

By God Himself
(Fifth Stage)

. . . that all the peoples of the earth may know that the LORD is God; there is no other. (1 Kings 8:60)

After these things the word of the LORD came to Abram in a vision, saying, "Do not be afraid, Abram. I am your shield, your exceedingly great reward." (Genesis 15:1)

And He said, "My Presence will go with you, and I will give you rest." (Exodus 33:14)

If there arises among you a prophet or a
dreamer of dreams, and he gives you a sign or a
wonder, and the sign or the wonder comes to
pass, of which he spoke to you, saying, "Let us
go after other gods"— which you have not known—
"and let us serve them," you shall not listen
to the words of that prophet or that dreamer
of dreams, for the LORD your God is testing you to
know whether you love the LORD your God with
all your heart and with all your soul. You shall
walk after the LORD your God and fear Him, and
keep His commandments and obey His voice;
you shall serve Him and hold fast to Him.
(Deuteronomy 13:1-4)

The LORD is my shepherd; I shall not want. He
makes me to lie down in green pastures; He
leads me beside the still waters. He restores
my soul; He leads me in the paths of righteousness
for His name's sake. (Psalm 23:1-3)

This is the goal on earth. In all we have touched upon
we have not approached the goal of the hereafter. God is
never in a hurry and His guidance is so severe and so simple, so sweet and so satisfying, that nothing but the child-
spirit can discern it. But this is the goal—God Himself.

> . . . nor joy, not peace,
> Nor even blessing, but Himself, my God.

How true is the word of the apostle Paul:
"Strengthened with all might, according to His glorious
power, for all patience and longsuffering with joy"

(Colossians 1:11). Our Lord Himself strikes the same note of patience: "By your patience possess your souls" (Luke 21:19), and the apostle John writes: "I, John, both your brother and companion in the tribulation and kingdom and patience of Jesus Christ . . ." (Revelation 1:9). Oh, the discipline of patience! How His guidance hastens us, sweetens us, and quickens us, until without let or hindrance He can guide us by Himself.

> Go thou into thy closet, shut thy door—
>   And pray to Him in secret: He will hear.
> But think not thou, by one wild bound, to clear
> The numberless ascensions, more and more,
> Of starry stairs that must be climbed, before
>   Thou comest to the Father's likeness near;
>   And bendest down to kiss His feet so dear
> That, step by step, their mounting flights passed o'er.
>   Be thou content if on thy weary need
> There falls a sense of showers and of the Spring;
> A hope that makes it possible to fling
>   Sickness aside, and go and do the deed:
>   For highest aspiration will not lead
> Unto the calm beyond all questioning.

From earliest childhood there has hovered over us the blessed presence that is indefinable. But it is only to the soul disciplined by suffering, by loneliness, and by divine guidance, that "our Father's feet" appear among the dusty clouds. In the days and years of the preparation of our moral and spiritual characters, the vision tarried and we wearied waiting for it. How often it seemed like some vagrant will-o'-the-wisp, and all life grew sick with longing. But ever and anon a vision came, perhaps in the rapt spell of a prayer, when one felt if he put out his hand he might, nay, he would, touch God Himself. Perhaps it was in a holy spell of contemplation that God Himself enfolded us, till fear was impossible, and God was all in all, beyond all language and all thought. But these all passed:

> God's fashion is another; day by day
> And year by year He tarrieth; little need
> The Lord should hasten; whom he loves the most
> He seeks not oftenest, nor woos him long,
> But by denial quickens his desire,
> And in forgetting best remembers him,
> Till that man's heart grows humble and reaches out
> To the least glimmer of the feet of God,
> Grass on the mountain-tops or the early note
> Of wild birds in the bush before the day,—
> Wherever sweetly in the ends of the earth
> Are fragments of a peace that knows not man.

What is the meaning of all the pain, the longing and the questioning? Why does God not tell us plainly of Himself? Ah! our God is a master workman in perfecting His ideas in us; He never hastens. So often we mistake Him and His purpose, and sink into quietism and contemplation. When we begin to repose in a sanctified stagnation, suddenly He ruthlessly uproots us, and when at last we are agreed with Him and His ways, He dazes and confounds us with His own questions. (All this is put for our instruction in the thirty-eighth chapter of the book of Job.) We do so want God to realize that we take ourselves very seriously. But some of the questions God asks us destroy this seriousness:

Where were you when I laid the foundations of the earth? . . . Have you commanded the morning since your days began, and caused the dawn to know its place, . . . Have you entered the springs of the sea? Or have you walked in search of its depths? Have the gates of death been revealed to you? Or have you seen the doors of the shadow of death? Have you comprehended the breadth of the earth? . . . Can you bind the cluster of the Pleiades, or loose the belt of Orion? Can you bring out Mazzaroth in its season? Or can you guide the Great Bear with its cubs? Do you know the ordinances of the heavens? Can you set their dominion over the earth?

Oh, these terrible questions when God seems to laugh at the soul, destroying its serious self-importance, even while He upholds that soul.

Then Job answered the LORD and said: "Behold, I am vile; what shall I answer You? I will lay my hand over my mouth. Once I have spoken, but I will not answer; yes, twice, but I will proceed no further . . . . I know that You can do every thing, and that no purpose of Yours can be withheld from You. You asked, 'Who is this who hides counsel without knowledge?' Therefore I have uttered what I did not understood, . . . I have heard of You by the hearing of the ear, but now my eye sees You. Therefore I abhor myself, and repent in dust and ashes." (See Job 39–42)

It is by these processes, for the most part unstateable, that God by His divine guidance destroys that awful barrier of taking ourselves too seriously.

Lord, what I once had done with youthful might,
Had I been from the first true to the truth,
Grant me, now old, to do—with better sight,
And humbler heart, if not the brain of youth;
So wilt thou, in thy gentleness and truth,
Lead back thy old soul, by the path of pain,
Round to his best—young eyes and heart and brain.

Come to me, Lord: I will not speculate how,
Nor think at which door I would have thee appear,
Nor put off calling till my floors be swept,
But cry, 'Come, Lord, come anyway, come now.'
Doors, windows, I throw wide; my head I bow,
And sit like some one who so long has slept
That he knows nothing till his life draws near.

God is a light so bright that the first vision of Him is
dark with excess of light. In Genesis 15, we read that "the
word of the LORD came to Abram in a vision," (note, it was
a vision—God's order is, first vision, then humiliation, then
reality) "saying, 'Do not be afraid, Abram: I am your shield,
and your exceedingly great reward.'. . . Now when the sun
was going down, a deep sleep fell upon Abram; and behold,
horror and great darkness fell upon him"—a darkness
through excess of light.

There is much that changes during this discipline of
divine guidance, but one thing grows clearer and clearer,
the revelation of God Himself. Moses, the servant of God,
was guided first by the cloudy pillar that is, by an outward
mysterious method; then by guidance from Mount Sinai
with its inner understanding of the words uttered there.
Then we see the God of the cloudy pillar, the God of

Mount Sinai's law, revealing Himself to him, and saying, "My Presence will go with you, and I will give you rest" (Exodus 33:14). The unspeakable rapture of it all made the heart of Moses plead, "Please, show me Your glory," and God in overflowing graciousness and condescension did so. "Here is a place by Me, and you shall stand on the rock . . . and you shall see My back; but My face shall not be seen" (Exodus 33:21–23).

"Here is a place by Me," a place of unapproachable safety. Affliction and tribulation may destroy all else, but the saint abiding in this secret place of the Most High is untouchable. There is no self-consciousness there, no uncertainty, but only rest, unfathomable rest in God Himself, not in a vision of God, but in God Himself as a reality, a living, bright reality. Walking with God and talking to Him as friend with friend, knowing that God knows He can do what He likes with us; there are no questions and no perplexities because He knows. Here, in the heart of this way of guidance by Himself, does God convey to us "the secret of the Lord."

> Within this place of certain good
>   Love evermore expands her wings,
> Or nestling in Thy perfect choice,
>   Abides content with what it brings.
>
> Oh, lightest burden, sweetest yoke!
>   It lifts, it bears my happy soul,
> It giveth wings to this poor heart;
>   My freedom is Thy grand control.
>
> Upon God's will I lay me down,
>   As child upon its mother's breast;
> No silken couch, nor softest bed,
>   Could ever give me such deep rest.

Thy wonderful, grand will, my God,
    With triumph now I make it mine;
And faith shall cry a joyous Yes!
    To every dear command of Thine.

A dear little friend of mine, not four years old, facing one day some big difficulty to her little heart, with a very wise shake of her head, said, "I'll go and tell my papa." Presently she came back, this time with every fiber of her little body strutting with the pride that shone in her eye, "Now, my papa's coming!" Presently her papa came, she clasped her little hands and screamed with delight, and danced round about him, unspeakably confident in her papa. Child of God, does something face you that terrifies your heart? Say, "I'll tell my Father." Then come back "boasting" in the Lord, "Now my Father's coming." And when He comes, you too will clasp your hands in rapture, your mouth will be filled with laughter, and you will be like one that dreams.

And all this seems immeasurable bliss here and now. What will it be when this order has passed away? If all this is but as His back, not His face, oh, what will it be! It has not entered into the heart of man to conceive!

Conclusion

The deep secret of God is love, and only the child-heart and the child-spirit can find the way to learn this secret. Jesus Christ satisfies the last aching abyss of the human spirit, and until He does there is a great element of the precarious in our lives. Half the heartbreaks in life are caused by the lack of understanding that

We needs must love the highest when we see it,
Not Lancelot, nor another.

Half the wasted days and languid reveries and immortal contemplations that embarrass human relationships and obliterate individual responsibility arise from the same lack of understanding. God is not an outward gush of sentiment, not a vague abstraction of impersonal good nature: God is a living, intense reality, and until this truth is grasped, the puzzles and the questions are more than can be met. But when by the discipline of His divine guidance, we know Him, and that His going with us gives us rest, then time and eternity are merged and lost in that amazingly vital relationship. The union is one not of mystic contemplation, but of intense perfection of activity; not the rest of the placid peace of stagnation, but the rest of perfect motion.

> Only, my God, see thou that I content thee—
> Oh, take thy own content upon me, God!
> Ah, never, never, sure, wilt thou repent thee
> That thou hast called thy Adam from the clod!
> Yet must I mourn that thou shouldst ever find me
> One moment sluggish, needing more of the rod
> Than thou didst think when thy desire designed me.

> No less than thou, O Father, do we need
> A God to friend each lonely one of us.

2

The Discipline of Suffering

Beloved, do not think it strange concerning the fiery trial which is to try you, as though some strange thing happened to you. . . . Therefore let those who suffer according to the will of God commit their souls to Him in doing good, as to a faithful Creator. (1 Peter 4:12, 19)

The awful problem of suffering continually crops up in the Scriptures and in life, and remains a mystery. From the time of Job until now, and from before Job, the mystery of suffering remains. And always, after the noisy clamor of the novice in suffering, and after the words of weight of the veteran; after the sarcasm and cynicism and bitterness of more or less pained people, aye, and after the slander of Satan against God—the voice of the Spirit sounds clear, "Have you considered My servant Job?" (Job 1:8).

Perhaps to be able to explain suffering is the clearest indication of never having suffered. Sin, suffering, and sanctification are not problems of the mind, but facts of life—mysteries that awaken all other mysteries until the heart rests in God, and waiting patiently knows "He does all things well." Oh, the unspeakable joy of knowing that God reigns! that He is our Father, and that the clouds are but "the dust of His feet"! Religious life is based and built up and matured on primal implicit trust, transfigured by love. The explicit statement of that life can only be made by the spectator, never by the saint.

Some years ago the wife of a murdered missionary in China told me of the blank amazed agony of those days—"We did not feel, we did not pray, we were dazed with sorrow." She was shown a lock of her little child's golden hair, and was told that both husband and child had been discovered murdered, beheaded, and naked in a godless Chinese town. Shattered and undone, the widow returned with the little ones spared to her to Britain. She did not doubt God, but—"He did not answer prayer. Oh, how many prayed for my husband, good valued servant of God, but all to no avail." In those days of dull dreary reaction the people who nearly drove her wild with distress were those who knew chapter and verse, the why and wherefore of her suffering and grief. She said, "I used to beat a tattoo on the floor with my foot while they chattered, crying in my heart, 'How long, O LORD, how long?'" One day as she lay prostrate on the sofa the old minister who had known her husband in happier days entered the room softly. He did not speak but came gently over to her and kissed her on the forehead and went out without saying a word. "From that moment," she said, "my heart began to heal."

The unexplained things in life are more than the explained. God seems careless as to whether people understand Him or not; He scarcely vindicates His saints to them. Martha and Mary tell Jesus of the sickness of Lazarus: "Lord, behold, he whom You love is sick" (John 11:3); but Jesus sends no word, nor does He go; Lazarus dies, is buried, and four days afterwards Jesus appears. If you do not understand Martha as she exclaims, in effect, "Why, I know that my brother will rise again at the last day, but that does not explain why You did not come when I sent for You; he need not have died if You had come"—if you do not understand Martha and are satisfied with any explanation to be deduced from this incident, you are unaware of the problem of suffering, unaware of the poignant agony of God's silences.

An informal consideration of 1 Peter 4:12–19 will serve to knit into some kind of order what we consider the Bible indicates and implies with regard to the discipline of suffering.

The Springs of Suffering

> But let none of you suffer as a murderer, a thief, an evildoer, or as a busybody in other people's matters. (verse 15)

The first spring of suffering from the Bible's point of view is twofold—wrongdoing and wrong temper.

Wrongdoing

> But let none of you suffer as a murderer, a thief, an evildoer.

The blasting blight of wrongdoing finds its expression in the literature of all the ages; it is a suffering that works as cruelly as the grave, and is as undying as the eternal ages. By way of expression to the suffering that springs from wrongdoing, Myers' words are final—

> When this man's best desire and highest aim
> Had ended in the deed of traitorous shame,
> When to his bloodshot eyes grew wild and dim
> The stony faces of the Sanhedrin—
> When in his rage he could no longer bear

Men's voices nor the sunlight nor the air,
Nor sleep, nor waking, nor his own quick breath,
Nor God in Heaven, nor anything but death—
I bowed my head, and through my fingers ran
Tears for the end of that Iscariot man,
Lost in the hopeless struggle of the soul
To make the done undone, the broken whole.

The sense of the irrevocable wrings the human spirit with the awful suffering of "what might have been." It begins its records in the far past, hoary with the ages, when Paradise was lost, and the cherubim with the circling fiery sword branded the life of Adam and Eve with "Nevermore, nevermore." It embraces that lonely murderer Cain, who in his undying pain cried out, "My punishment is greater than I can bear" (Genesis 4:13). It pauses around Esau when, too late, remorse seized that strong man and made him weep those tears of bitter repentance, all in vain; and its records of the unspeakable suffering of the wrongdoer remain till today—

Oh, brother! howsoever, whereso'er
Thou hidest now the hell of thy despair,
Hear that one heart can pity, one can know
With thee thy hopeless, solitary woe.

F. W. H. Myers

Wrong Temper

There is also suffering that springs from the wrong tem-per—"But let none of you suffer . . . as a busybody in other people's matters" (1 Peter 4:15). From talking in the wrong mood springs a suffering so keen, so stinging, so belittling, so hopeless, that it debases and drives the suffering one still lower. The old song from the ancient pilgrim's song book has this thorn at the heart of its suffering—

> Deliver my soul, O LORD, from lying lips, and from a deceitful tongue. What shall be given to you, or what shall be done to you, you false tongue? Sharp arrows of the warrior, with coals of the broom tree! (Psalm 120:2–4)

The suffering which springs from "being a busybody in other people's matters" is humiliating to the last degree. A free translation of 1 Thessalonians 4:11 might well read: "Study to shut up and mind your own business," and among all the texts we hang on our walls, let this be one. The suffering that arises from a wrong temper has no refining side, but only a humiliating side. "Therefore take heed to your spirit" (Malachi 2:15). A blameworthy temper of mind is the most damning thing in the human soul. Peter, as a meddler in other men's matters, received a deserved rebuke from our Lord: "Peter, seeing him [John], said to Jesus, 'But Lord, what about this man?' Jesus said to him, 'If I will that he remain till I come, what is that to you? You follow Me' " (John 21:21–22). And surely the rebuke contained in our Lord's answer to Martha is of the same nature: "Martha, Martha, you are worried and troubled about many things. But one thing is needed, and Mary has chosen that good part, which will not be taken away from her" (Luke 10:41–42), that is, "She is taking her orders from Me."

How will sad memory point where, here and there,
    Friend after Friend, by falsehood or by fate,
From him or from each other parted were,

And love sometimes becomes the nurse of hate! . . .
Rather, he thinks he held not duly dear
    Love, the best gift that Man on Man bestows,
While round his downward path, recluse and drear,
    He feels the chill indifferent shadows close.
"Why did I not," his spirit murmurs deep,
    "At every cost of the momentary pride,
Preserve the love for which in vain I weep;
    Why had I wish or hope or sense beside?
O cruel issue of some selfish thought!
    O long, long echo of some angry tone!
O fruitless lesson, mercilessly taught,
    Alone to linger—and to die alone!"

Houghton

The wreck of many friendships has started in this mutiny of busybody meddling. Suffering "as a busybody" and listening to slander ends in pitiable pain. This wrong temper slanders the Almighty, and people believe the busybody gossip of the devil and sever friendship with God. Oh, the damnable pangs caused by that arch busybody, "the accuser of the brethren."

This then is the first spring of suffering, and the Spirit warns people lest they drink of this spring and endure a suffering that is neither grand nor ennobling.

Suffering as a Christian

But if yet anyone suffers as a Christian, let him not be ashamed, but let him glorify God in this matter. (1 Peter 4:16)

The suffering that arises from superiority, from an essential difference from the societies around, is an ennobling and God-glorifying thing. Our designation of "Christian" is of divine appointment, whether it comes from the versatile wit of Antioch or from the reverent respect of the Gentile; to live worthily of the name of Christian is to suffer persecution. To suffer because of meekness is an exalting, refining and God-glorifying suffering. And mark this and mark it well—to "suffer as a Christian" is a shameful thing in the eyes of the societies of this world. The friends who, in your hour of trial and slander gather round to support and stand with you, are first amazed, then dazed, and then disgusted, when they find that you really do not mean to stand up for yourself, but meekly to submit. In that hour when your friends pity you (Oh, the shame of being pitied, says the world; but what a God-glorifying thing it is, for to be pitied by the world is to be pitied by God) He Himself will come and whisper to your spirit—"Blessed are you when men hate you, and when they exclude you, and revile you, and cast out your name as evil, for the Son of Man's sake. Rejoice in that day and leap for joy! For indeed your reward is great in heaven" (Luke 6:22–23).

To "suffer as a Christian" is not to be marked peculiar because of your views, or because you will not bend to conventionality; these things are not Christian, but ordinary human traits from which all people suffer irrespective of creed or religion or no religion. To "suffer as a Christian" is to suffer because there is an essential difference between you and the world which rouses the contempt of the world, and the disgust and hatred of the spirit that is in the world. To "suffer as a Christian" is to have no answer when the world's satire is turned on you, as it was turned on Jesus Christ when He hung upon the cross, when they turned His words into jest and jeer. They will do the same to you. He gave no answer, neither can you.

"If anyone suffers as a Christian, let him not be

ashamed." It was in the throes of this binding, amazing problem that Peter staggered. Peter meant to go with his Lord to death, and he did go; but never at any moment did he imagine that he would have to go without Him—that he would see Jesus taken by the power of the world, "led as a lamb to the slaughter," and have no answer, no word to explain—that froze him to the soul. That is what it means to "suffer as a Christian"—to hear people taunt Him, see them tear His words to pieces and feel you cannot answer; to smart under their merciless, pitying sarcasm because you belong to that contemptible sect of "Christians." When the heart is stung in the first moments of such suffering the language of the poet may suit it—

I can simply wish I might refute you,
    Wish my friend would,—by a word, a wink,—
Bid me stop that foolish mouth,—you brute, you!
    He keeps absent,—why, I cannot think.

Never mind! Though foolishness may flout me,
    One thing's sure enough: 'tis neither frost,
No, nor fire, shall freeze or burn from out me
    Thanks for truth—though falsehood, gained—
        though lost.

Browning

But when you have been comforted by "His rod and His staff," you count it all joy to go through this God-glorifying suffering. "Let him glorify God in this matter." Suffering "as a Christian" is the second great spring of suffering, whose waters purify and ennoble the soul.

How very hard it is to be
A Christian! Hard for you and me,

And the sole thing that I remark
Upon this difficulty, this;
We do not see it where it is,
At the beginning of the race:
As we proceed, it shifts its place,
And where we looked for crowns to fall,
We find the tug's to come,—that's all.

. . . and I find it hard
To be a Christian, as I said!
Still every now and then my head
Raised glad, sinks mournful—all grows drear
Spite of the sunshine, . . .

But Easter Day breaks! But
Christ rises! Mercy every way
Is infinite—and who can say?

Browning

Suffering According to the Will of God
Therefore let those who suffer according to the
will of God commit their souls to Him in doing
good, as to a faithful Creator. (1 Peter 4:19)

If the springs of suffering we have been considering
arise in mystery, this spring overwhelms its own source
in mystery, as well as the soul it covers. The great tides
lift here, the splendid solitude of God's purpose transfigures agony into redemption and the baffling hurricanes
speed the soul like a flaming arrow on to God's great day.

G. K. Chesterton, writing on Job, says in his own individual, sufficient way—

> But God comforts Job with indecipherable mystery, and for the first time Job is comforted. Eliphaz gives one answer, Job gives another answer, and the question still remains an open wound. God simply refuses to answer, and somehow the question is settled. Job flings at God one riddle, God flings back at Job a hundred riddles, and Job is at peace; he is comforted with conundrums.

When all the trite things, the sentimental things, the poetic things and the explanatory things have been said, the still small voice of the Spirit introduces the perpetual conundrum—"Have you considered my servant Job?" And after a pause, when our commonplace shoes are off our feet and we stand before the Cross, the conundrum is put still more deeply and more perplexingly, "You are My beloved Son, in whom I am well pleased" (Mark 1:11). "Yet it pleased the LORD to bruise Him; He has put Him to grief" (Isaiah 53:10), and we bow the head while the spirit murmurs, "Who has believed our report [that which we have heard]? And to whom has the arm of the LORD been revealed?" (Isaiah 53:1).

This spring of suffering, suffering "according to the will of God," is a great deep. Job did not know the preface to his own story, neither does anyone. Job was never told that God and the devil had made a battleground of his soul. Job's suffering was not for his own sake, not for his perfecting or purifying. That was incidental. Job suffered "according to the will of God."

When shall we learn that God's great work is the production of saints? It is humbling beyond words to be told by our Father that it was not for love of the truth that we had been bold, but that the great labor allowed us was the means of releasing our imprisoned hearts and was for our own peace. God seems careless over what people do at times.

The words of our Lord sound from those blessed Palestinian days with a deeper, truer significance: "If anyone desires to come after Me, let him deny himself, and take up his cross daily, and follow Me," that is, I must never do God's will according to my will. That surely is the very essence of Satan's temptation of our Lord, and of every sanctified soul—"Take your right to yourself and do God's will according to your own sanctified understanding of it." "Never!" said Jesus, "For I have come down from heaven not to do My own will, but the will of Him who sent Me" (John 6:38). In the hour when dilemma perplexes him, the waves and the billows overwhelm him, and the noise of the waterspouts deafen him, the disciple learns the meaning of his Master's "Follow Me."

In the course of a sermon preached by Father Frere in St. Paul's Cathedral some years ago, "The Fourfold Attitude Towards Suffering," he said this:

> Have you, I wonder, ever had to do something to a pet dog in order to get it well, something which hurt it very much—pulled a thorn out of its foot, or washed out a wound, or anything of that sort? If so, you will remember the expression of dumb eloquence in the eyes of the dog as he looked at you; what you were doing hurt him tremendously and yet there seemed to speak from his eyes such a trust of you as if he would say, "I don't in the least understand what you are doing, what you are doing hurts, but go on with it."

That is an apt illustration of suffering "according to the will of God." It is very necessary to be brought to the stage of trust in our experience of suffering; perhaps we are brought to it most acutely when (in the case of someone we love) we have to look up mutely to God and say, "I don't understand it at all, but go on with what You are doing." That marks a real stage of learning to trust in God, and it is a step towards something still further on. Spiritual experience has begun; suffering has already deepened the soul. To look on at suffering with eyes that know not God is to make the mouth slander the Highest. To sympathize with people who suffer, without first knowing God, is to hate Him.

> Therefore gird up thyself, and come to stand
> Unflinching under the unfaltering hand,
> That waits to prove thee to the uttermost.
> It were not hard to suffer by His hand,
> If thou couldst see His face;—but in the dark!
> That is the one last trial:—be it so.
> Christ was forsaken, so must thou be too:
> How couldest thou suffer but in seeming, else?
> Thou wilt not see the face nor feel the hand,
> Only the cruel crushing of the feet,
> When through the bitter night the Lord comes down
> To tread the winepress.—Not by sight, but faith,
> Endure, endure,—be faithful to the end
>
> H. Hamilton King

The Signs of Suffering

People betray their suffering in different ways—by threatening and evildoing, by sullenness and quietism, or by actively doing good.

In the cruel fire of Sorrow
    Cast thy heart, do not faint or wail!
Let thy hand be firm and steady,
    Do not let thy spirit quail!
But wait till the trial is over

    And take thy heart again;
For as gold is tried by fire
    So a heart must be tried by pain.

I shall know by the gleam and glitter
    Of the golden chain you wear,
By your heart's calm strength in loving.
    Of the fire they have had to bear.
Beat on, true heart, forever!
    Shine bright, strong golden chain,
And bless the cleansing fire
    And the furnace of living pain!

A. Procter

Suffering, when the heart knows nothing of trust in God and love for the Highest, shows itself in rancorous spite and evil deeds. The sarcasms, the cynicisms, the satires, the slanders, the murders, the wars, the law suits, all these spring from this source, and are usually, although not always, the sign of suffering which springs from wrongdoing. When we sum up the history of the various civilizations whose records are available, we find it made up mostly of these forms of suffering, and we are reminded of the voice of the Ancient of Days echoing down the ages: "in toil [sorrow—KJV] shall you eat of it all the days of your life" (Genesis 3:17). It is caught up in the reflections of the wisest person that ever lived: "For all his days are sorrowful, and his work burdensome; even in the night his heart takes no rest" (Ecclesiastes 2:23); and uttered again in connection with God's servant Job, who remains the incarnation of the problem of suffering: "For affliction does not come from the dust, nor does trouble spring from the ground; yet man is born to trouble, as the sparks fly upward" (Job 5:67).

Suffering is the heritage of the bad, of the penitent, and of the Son of God. Each one ends in the cross. The bad thief is crucified, the penitent thief is crucified, and the Son of God is crucified. By these signs we know the widespread heritage of suffering.

> Judge not! the workings of his brain
>   And of his heart thou canst not see;
> What looks to thy dim eyes a stain,
>   In God's pure light may only be
> A scar, brought from some well-won field—
> Where thou wouldst only faint and yield.
>
> The look, the air that frets thy sight,
>   May be a token, that below
> The soul has closed in deadly fight
>   With some infernal fiery foe,
> Whose glance would scorch thy smiling grace,
> And cast thee shuddering on thy face!
>
> The fall thou darest to despise,—
>   May be the Angel's slackened hand
> Has suffered it, that he may rise
>   And take a firmer, surer stand;
> Or, trusting less to earthly things,
> May henceforth learn to use his wings.

So judge none lost but wait and see,
    With hopeful pity, not disdain!
The depth of the abyss may be
    The measure of the height of pain,
And love and glory that may raise
This soul to God in after days.

A. Procter

Another sign of suffering is characterized by sullenness and quietism. There is a luxury of suffering that fosters the growth of the most dangerous isolation of pride, and produces a kind of human sphinx shrouded in mystery, which seems more profound than it is. This luxury of suffering is preeminently cowardly as well as proud, its habit is the habit of the cloister or nunnery. According to the character of the individual, it is sullen and gloomy in its expression, or mystical and remote in its quietism. The portrayal of the sullen type is well expressed in Psalm 106:24–25. "Then they despised the pleasant land; they did not believe His word, but complained in their tents, and did not heed the voice of the LORD."

Bishop Paget in a remarkable essay on "The Sin of Accidie" deals with this suffering in a unique exposition of the sullen temperament; and the apostle Paul uses a significant phrase in the same connection: "the sorrow of the world produces death" (2 Corinthians 7:10). The ultimate result of this kind of suffering is a hatred of holier lives: "And all the congregation said to stone them with stones" (Numbers 14:10); envy and murmuring at the messengers of God: "They envied Moses in the camp, and Aaron the saint of the LORD" (Psalm 106:16); and sullen contempt of God's Word. Dante places these souls in the fifth circle, tormented in the Stygian lake—

Fix'd in the slime, they say: "Sad once were we,
In the sweet air made gladsome by the sun,
Carrying a foul and lazy mist within:
Now in these murky settlings are we sad."

The other aspect of this sign of suffering is different in character and quality, namely, quietism, a life spent in luxury or reverie and contemplation. This type of suffering was very common in medieval Christianity. It produces a quietness apart, and flatly contradicts the very spirit of Christianity. The psalmist of old tried to be a quietist, but he found himself too robust. It would not work with him: "I said, 'I will guard my ways, lest I sin with my tongue; I will restrain my mouth with a muzzle, while the wicked are before me.' I was mute with silence, I held my peace even from good; and my sorrow was stirred up. My heart was hot within me; while I was musing, the fire burned; then I spoke with my tongue" (Psalm 39:1–3). This kind of sanctity, so called, is highly esteemed in all religions, but it engenders a pseudomysticism that inevitably ends in private illuminations apart from the written Word and prayer, and actually spells "strong delusions." The true element in evangelical mysticism, which is easily distinguishable from quietism, is the mystery of a human life visibly "manifesting the life of the Lord Jesus in its mortal flesh."

This brings us to the third sign of suffering—actively doing good. "Therefore let those who suffer according to the will of God commit their souls to Him in doing good, as to a faithful Creator" (1 Peter 4:19). The New Testament idea of a saint is not a cloistered sentiment gathering around the head of an individual like a halo of glory, but a holy character reacting on life in deeds of holiness. "I am the true vine, and My Father is the vinedresser. Every branch in Me that does not bear fruit He takes away; and every branch that bears fruit He prunes, that it may bear more fruit" (John 15:1–2). The cleansing of the individual branch is here made the sign of doing good.

When a soul experiences suffering caused by the cleansing process and the pruning knife, he knows he is bearing fruit. A subtle law, which is ever and anon lost sight of by Christian teachers, is that an emotion which does not react in a proper manner will find an outlet in an improper manner. How often religious fervor and emotion, not finding reaction in its proper sphere, has sought an outlet in a lower, baser form. How sad and sordid and sorrowful is the connection between high spiritual emotions and sensual disaster. The hugging to one's self of any spiritual emotion is eminently dangerous.

This line of thought throws an important sidelight on our Lord's interview with Mary Magdalene on the resurrection morning. Mary thought to hold Jesus to herself, to have Him again as a blessed companion for herself, but Jesus said to her: "Do not cling to Me, for I have not yet ascended to My Father; but go to My brethren and say to them, 'I am ascending to My Father and your Father, and to My God and your God" (John 20:17). There, as ever, the emphasis is on doing, not on contemplation. Du Bose says:

> In the first place, Jesus took definite part with the West against the East in making the distinctive note of life not *apatheia* but *energeia*. Thought, desire, will, were not to be abjured and disowned in despair, through the overpowering sense of their futility. Life was not to be reduced to zero through their renunciation, but raised to infinity through their affirmation and satisfaction. The life of

Christianity is a life of infinite energy because it is a life of infinite faith and hope. (*The Gospel in the Gospels*)

The essential difference between the stoic and the saint is just at the point where they seem most alike. Dr. George Matheson points this out in his book entitled *Studies in the Portrait of Christ.* A stoic overcomes the world by passionlessness; the saint's overcoming is by passion. This suffering in actively doing good results in a blessed and beneficent reaction on life.

Arise! this day shall shine forevermore,
To thee a star divine on Time's dark shore!

Till now thy soul has been all glad and gay;
Bid it awake and look at Grief today! . . .

But now the stream has reached a dark, deep sea;
And Sorrow, dim and crowned, is waiting thee.

Each of God's soldiers bears a sword divine:
Stretch out thy trembling hands today for thine! . . .

Then with slow, reverent step, and beating heart,
From out thy joyous day thou must depart,—

And leaving all behind come forth alone,
To join the chosen band around the throne:—

Raise up thine eyes!—be Strong!—nor cast away
The crown that God has given thy soul today!

A. Proctor

Suffering "according to the will of God"—to be in "the will of God" is not a matter of intellectual discernment, but a state of the heart. To a sanctified soul the will of God is its implicit life, as natural as breathing. It is the sick person who knows intellectually what health is, and a sinful one knows intellectually what the will of God is. But a sanctified heart is the expression of the will of God. Its motto is: "My Father can do what He likes with me. He may bless me to death, or give me a bitter cup; I delight to do His will."

"As to a faithful Creator." The sovereignty of God is the greatest comfort to the saint. The soul of the sanctified saint is *en rapport* with God. He has no responsibility—he is "without care" because his Father cares. God's predestinations are that soul's voluntary choosings. The preeminent mystery in this thought is the mystery of the nature of love: the saint knows, with a knowledge "which passes knowledge." This truth is never discerned by the powerful in intellect, but only by the pure in heart.

> Therefore to whom turn I but to thee, the ineffable
>   Name?
>   Builder and maker, thou, of houses not made with
>   hands!
> What, have fear of change from thee who art ever the
>   same?
>   Doubt that thy power can fill the heart that thy
>   power expands?
> There shall never be one lost good! What was, shall
>   live as before;
>   The evil is null, is nought, is silence implying
>   sound;
> What was good shall be good, with, for evil, so much
>   good more;

On the earth the broken arcs; in the heaven, a
    perfect round.
All we have willed or hoped or dreamed of good shall
    exist;
    Not its semblance, but itself; no beauty, nor good,
        nor power
Whose voice has gone forth, but each survives for the
    melodist
    When eternity affirms the conception of an hour.
The high that proved too high, the heroic for earth too
    hard,
    The passion that left the ground to lose itself in the
        sky,
Are music sent up to God by the lover and the bard;
    Enough that he heard it once: we shall hear it by-
        and-by.

Browning

This brings us to the grand finale of the discipline of suffering, namely:

The Sublimity of Suffering

It is not possible to define life, or love, or suffering, for
the words are but names for incalculable elements in human
experience, the very essence of which is implicit, not explicit.
To quote G. K. Chesterton again:

A critic who takes a scientific view of the Book of
Job is exactly like a surgeon who should take a poeti-
cal view of appendicitis; he is simply an old "muddler."

Suffering is grand when the heart is right with God. But
for the night "the moon and the stars, which You have
ordained" (Psalm 8:3), would never be seen. And so God
gives to His own "the treasures of darkness."

The sublimity of suffering can be indicated in three glorious outlines—Friendship with God, Fellowship with Jesus, and Freedom in the Highest.

Friendship with God.
> Greater love has no one than this, than to lay down one's life for his friends. You are My friends if you do whatever I command you. (John 15:13–14)

The relationship of a soul to Jesus Christ is capable of being interpreted in varying ways, but our Lord seems to imply that there is an end to discipleship, an end to learning the pace. A point is reached where the disciple emerges as the friend of God, carrying with him the swinging stride of the mountains of God, and the atmosphere of the eternal hills. In such glimpses one recalls how in the dawnlight of the ages "Enoch walked with God" and so fascinating, so exhilarating, so entrancing, were those walks that one day he did not return—"and he was not, for God took him." Again, we read of Abraham, who has been known through all the ages as the "friend of God," the father of all those who have become or will yet become the friends of God.

It is not possible to express what Jesus Christ has done for us in better words than those of the writer to the Hebrews: "For it was fitting for Him, for whom are all things and by whom are all things, in bringing many sons to glory, to make the captain of their salvation perfect through sufferings. For both He who sanctifies and those who are being sanctified are all of one, for which reason He is not ashamed to call them brethren" (Hebrews 2:10–11). Oh, unspeakably blessed is the suffering of the sanctified that leads them step by step to this sublime friendship with God!

But whoso wants God only and lets life go,
Seeks him with sorrow and pursues him far,
And finds him weeping, and in no long time
Again the High and Unapproachable
Evanishing escapeth, and that man
Forgets the life and struggle of the soul,
Falls from his hope, and dreams it was a dream

Yet back again perforce with sorrow and shame
Who once hath known him must return, nor long
Can cease from loving, nor endures alone
The dreadful interspace of dreams and day,
Once quick with God; nor is content as those
Who look into each other's eyes and seek
To find one strong enough to uphold the earth,
Or sweet enough to make it heaven: abba,
Whom seek they or whom find? for in all the world
There is none by thee, my God, there is none but thee.

F. W. H. Myers

Lest you who are suffering under the call to supreme sanctification should faint or wail, you will presently hear Him say, "Do not be afraid. I am your shield, and your exceedingly great reward" (see Genesis 15:1). Do you catch the majesty, the might, the awe, the unspeakable satisfaction of those words?

My goal is God Himself, not joy, nor peace,
    Nor even blessing, but Himself, my God;
'Tis His to lead me there, not mine, but His—
    "At any cost, dear Lord, by any road."

F. Brook

Oh, that people would not degrade and belittle what our Lord Jesus Christ has done for us by morbid introspective sympathy with one another! How many of us can hear Him say: "These things I have spoken to you in figurative language; but the time is coming when I will no longer speak to you in figurative language, but I will tell you plainly about the Father. In that day you will ask in My name, and I do not say to you that I shall pray the Father for you; for the Father Himself loves you, because you have loved Me, and have believed that I came forth from God" (John 16:25–27). Friendship with God is not a legal fiction; it is a reality in time. "In Your presence is fullness of joy; at your right hand there are pleasures forevermore" (Psalm 16:11).

And all this is ours by the sheer might of the atonement of Jesus, who gave Himself for us to cleanse and recreate us, to baptize us with the Holy Spirit and fire, till looking at us as we tread this earth among the common round and tasks of human beings, Jesus will see of the travail of His soul, and being satisfied, will say, "Father, this have I done; here is another soul." That soul incandescent with the Holy Spirit, walks and talks with God, as friend with friend, letting God do as He wills with him. This, and nothing less and nothing else, constitutes the suffering of the sanctified. Oh, the sublimity of the sufferings of the sanctified! Suffering according to the will of God, not so much for personal perfecting as to enable God to express His ideas in the life.

Fellowship with Jesus

But if, impatient, thou let slip thy cross,
Thou wilt not find it in this world again,
Nor in another; here, and here alone
Is given thee to *suffer* for God's sake.
In other worlds we shall more perfectly
Serve Him and love Him, praise Him, work for Him,

Grow near and nearer Him with all delight;
But then we shall not any more be called
To suffer, which is our appointment here.
Couldst thou not suffer then one hour,—or two
If He should call thee from thy cross today.
Saying, It is finished!—that hard cross of thine
From which thou prayest for deliverance,
Thinkest thou not some passion of regret
Would overcome thee? Thou wouldst say, "So soon?
Let me go back, and suffer yet awhile
More patiently;—I have not yet praised God."
And He might answer to thee,—"Never more.
All pain is done with." Whenso'er it comes,
That summons that we look for, it will seem
Soon, yea too soon. Let us take heed in time
That God may now be glorified in us;
And while we suffer, let us set our souls
To suffer perfectly; since this alone,
The suffering, which is this world's special grace,
May here be perfected and left behind.

H. Hamilton King

The Cross of Jesus Christ stands unique and alone. His Cross is not our cross. Our cross is that we manifest before the world the fact that we are sanctified to do nothing but the will of God. By means of His Cross, our cross becomes our divinely appointed privilege. It is necessary to emphasize this because there is so much right feeling and wrong teaching abroad on the subject. We are never called upon to carry Christ's Cross: His Cross is the center of time and eternity; the answer to the enigmas of both.

"For to this you were called, because Christ also suffered for us, leaving us an example, that you should follow

His steps" (1 Peter 2:21). This is the essence of fellowship with His sufferings. "He suffered for you." Are you suffering on account of someone else, or for someone else? Are your agonizing prayers and suffering before the Lord in behalf of that "distressing case" because it hurts you, discomforts you, makes you long for release? If so, you are not in fellowship with His suffering, nor anything like it. But if your soul, out of love for God, longs for others and bears with them in a voluntary, vicarious way, then you have a fellowship divine indeed.

When your work suffers eclipse do you wail before God because the work of your hands is ruined? Do you say, "I looked upon this as my lifework, now it is broken and blighted and shattered?" If so, you do not know what fellowship with His suffering means. But if, when you see people defiling the house of God, making His courts a place for traffic in worldly business and engendering false affections, a home for vagrant beasts, you agonize before the Lord with alternate zeal and tears, then you have fellowship with Him in His sufferings. "I now rejoice in my sufferings for you, and fill up in my flesh what is lacking in the afflictions of Christ, for the sake of His body, which is the church" (Colossians 1:24).

"For as the sufferings of Christ abound in us, so our consolation also abounds through Christ" (2 Corinthians 1:5).

"That I may know Him and the power of His resurrection, and the fellowship of His sufferings, being conformed to His death" (Philippians 3:10).

This fellowship with His sufferings is a mystery only understood by the saint. But not all suffering leads to this sublime fellowship. To suffer from the hatred of other people, to be separated from their company, to be reproached by society, to be considered as having an evil name, is not necessarily to have fellowship with His sufferings. We only have fellowship with Him if we suffer "for the Son of Man's sake." To suffer martyrdom, to lose your life, to leave father and mother, houses and lands, is not to have fellowship with His sufferings unless it is done because of Him and for His sake.

This same thing thins the ranks of the suffering ones who claim fellowship with Him, and it humbles us to the dust. To drink of His cup, to be baptized with His baptism, is a thing so rare that few of us ever see it, or enter into it. Have you begun the solitary way with Him and has the clamor of father or mother made you quail? Or does love for them pale into insignificance before your love for Him. Does your spouse arise, and with face and hands too tender, seek to prevent you from your course for Him? Or does your love for Him in that supreme moment rise so high that your love for him or her appears hatred in comparison? Have your children's baby fingers bowed your head to earth again? Or has your love for Him prevailed, and commending them, bone of your bone, and flesh of your flesh, to God, have you gone forth? Have brothers and sisters scathed and scandalized you, shamed you by their just and righteous indignation? Or has love for Him prevailed even over that? Has self-culture impeded your solitary way with Him? Or has love for Him been so passionate that you love not your own life? Then you have become a disciple of Jesus indeed.

All this is not yet fellowship with His sufferings; it is the first lesson learned towards that fellowship: "If anyone comes to Me and does not hate his father and mother, wife and children, brothers and sisters, yes, and his own life also, he cannot be My disciple" (Luke 14:26). " 'Does this offend you?'. . . From that time many of His disciples went back and walked with Him no more. Then Jesus said to the twelve, 'Do you also want to go away?' " (John 6:61, 67).

Oh, the sublimity of the suffering that gains us fellowship with Jesus!

> To abandon all, to strip one's self of all, in order to seek and follow Jesus Christ naked to Bethlehem, where He was born, naked to the hall where He was scourged, and naked to Calvary where He died on the cross, is so great a mystery that neither the thing, nor the knowledge of it, is given to any but through faith in the Son of God.
>
> *John Wesley*

Wherever this finds you, my beloved sister or brother, can you hear, in imagination at least, our Lord say to you at the last, knowing all, "Well done, good and faithful servant"?

> But if Himself He came to thee, and stand
> Beside thee, gazing down on thee with eyes
> That smile, and suffer; that will smite thy heart,
> With their own pity, to a passionate peace;
> And reach to thee Himself the Holy Cup,
> (With all its wreathen stems of passionflowers
> And quivering sparkles of the ruby stars),
> Pallid and royal, saying, "Drink with Me";
> Wilt thou refuse? Nay, not for Paradise!
> —The pale brow will compel thee, the pure hands
> Will minister unto thee; thou shalt take
> Of that communion through the solemn depths
> Of the dark waters of thine agony,
> With heart that praises Him, that yearns to Him

The closer through that hour. Hold fast His hand,
Though the nails pierce thine too! take only care
Lest one drop of the sacramental wine
Be spilled, of that which ever shall unite
Thee, soul and body to thy living Lord!

For the glory and the passion of this midnight,
    I praise Thy name, I give Thee thanks, O Christ!
Thou that hast neither failed me nor forsaken,
    Through these hard hours with victory overpriced;
Now that I too of Thy passion have partaken,
    For the world's sake called, elected, sacrificed.

Thou wast alone through Thy redemption-vigil,
    Thy friends had fled;
The angel at the garden from Thee parted,
    And solitude instead,
More than the scourge, or cross, O tenderhearted,
    Under the crown of thorns bowed down Thy head.

But I, amid the torture, and the taunting,
    I have had Thee!
Thy hand was holding my hand fast and faster,
    Thy voice was close to me,
And glorious eyes said, "Follow Me, thy Master,
    Smile as I smile thy faithfulness to see."

                    H. Hamilton King

Freedom in the Highest

    Freedom is that implicit life which fulfills all the law of God and transfigures the fulfillment in loving devotion. Oh, the sublimity of that freedom in the highest, wherein suffering has freed us from being the dupes of ourselves, of our convictions, and our temperaments, and we realize that "our fellowship is with the Father and with his Son Jesus Christ" (1 John 1:3).

Let it be said with reverence, even with bated breath and in the atmosphere of the deepest humility, that suffering "according to the will of God" raises us to a freedom and felicity in the highest that baffles all language to express. As ever, the only sufficient language is the language of Scripture: "If anyone loves Me, he will keep My word; and My Father will love him, and We will come to him and make Our home with him" (John 14:23). "If anyone hears My voice and opens the door, I will come in to him and dine with him, and he with Me" (Revelation 3:20). This is verily the apotheosis of freedom and felicity. This mirrors the incomprehensible mystery of the abiding of the Trinity in every suffering soul raised to the sublimity of fellowship. "Therefore if the Son makes you free, you shall be free indeed" (John 8:36). "I sat down in his shade with great delight, and his fruit was sweet to my taste. He brought me to the banqueting house, and his banner over me was love" (Song of Solomon 2:3–4). "Today I must stay at your house" (Luke 19:5).

Do you know the unspeakable bliss of Father, Son, and Holy Spirit abiding with you, feasting with you, and making you one with them? This is the sublime height of suffering "according to the will of God."

Surely we gaze now at the mystery of godliness. No wonder "angels desire to look into these things." A poor, evilly-disposed sinner is cleansed, saved, wholly sanctified, walking as the friend of God, in communion with the Lord in suffering, and the Trinity abiding with him as companions daily and hourly and momentarily. This truly is a height from which the soul can look into the depths of the pain that our Savior and sanctifier went through to bring us there. This gives us a key to understand the shame and agony, the mock trial, the crucifixion, the resurrection, the ascension, and Pentecost.

> There is a way for man to rise
>   To that sublime abode;
> An offering and a sacrifice,
> A Holy Spirit's energies,
>   An advocate with God.

No wonder the apostle Paul prays "that the God of our Lord Jesus Christ, the Father of glory, may give to you the spirit of wisdom and revelation in the knowledge of Him, the eyes of your understanding being enlightened; that you may know what is the hope of His calling, what are the riches of the glory of His inheritance in the saints" (Ephesians 1:17–18). This is the hope of *His* calling; we are part of the glory of *His* inheritance. This unveils to our hearts an understanding of our Lord's great prayer "that they may be one just as We are one" (John 17:22). One in holiness, one in love, one forever with God the Father, God the Son, and God the Holy Spirit.

> Servants of God!—or sons
> Shall I not call you? because
> Not as servants ye knew
> Your Father's innermost mind
> His, who unwillingly sees
> One of His little ones lost—
> Yours is the praise, if mankind
> Hath not as yet in its march
> Fainted, and fallen, and died.

Then, in such hour of need
Of your fainting, dispirited race,
Ye, like angels appear,
Radiant with ardour divine.
Beacons of hope, ye appear!
Languor is not in your heart,
Weakness is not in your word,
Weariness not on your brow.
Ye alight in our van! at your voice,
Panic, despair, flee away.
Ye move through the ranks, recall
The stragglers, refresh the outworn,
Praise, reinspire the brave.

Order, courage, return;
Eyes rekindling, and prayers,
Follow your steps as ye go.
Ye fill up the gaps in our files,
Strengthen the wavering line,
Stablish, continue our march,
On, to the bound of the waste,
On, to the City of God.

Matthew Arnold

But, marvel of marvels, the outward and visible sign of the sublimity of friendship and fellowship and freedom in the Highest is in being the humblest servant of all: "Let this mind be in you which was also in Christ Jesus, who, being in the form of God did not consider it robbery to be equal with God, but made Himself of no reputation, taking the form of a bondservant, and coming in the likeness of men," (Philippians 2:5-7). "By this all will know that you are My disciples" (John 13:35).

It is a strange thing, a unique thing, that in this hierarchy of suffering, those nearest the throne are willingly, eagerly, the humblest; and the King Himself is Servant of all. "I am among you as the One who serves" (Luke 22:27).

"Its way of suffering is the witness which a soul bears to itself" (Amiel).

The production of a saint is the grandest thing earth can give to heaven. A saint is not a person with a saintly character: a saint *is* a saintly character. Character, not ecstatic moods, is the stuff of saintliness. A saint is a living epistle written by the finger of God, known and read of all people. A saint may be any person, any wastrel or vagabond, who discovering himself at Calvary, with the nature of sin uncloaked, lies in despair; then discerning Jesus Christ as the substitute for sin and rising in the glamour of amazement, he cries out: "Jesus, I should be there." And to his astonished spirit, he receives justification from all his sinfulness by that wondrous atonement. Then, standing in that great light, and placing his hands, as it were, over his Savior's crucified hands, his feet over His crucified feet, he crucifies forever his right to himself. And the Lord baptizes him with the Holy Spirit and fire; substituting in him a new principle of life, an identity of holiness with Himself, until he bears unmistakably a family likeness to Jesus Christ.

God, who at sundry times in manners many
    Spake to the fathers and is speaking still,
Eager to find if ever or if any
    Souls will obey and hearken to his will;—

Who that one moment has the least descried him,
    Dimly and faintly, hidden and afar,
Doth not despise all excellence beside him,
    Pleasures and powers that are not and that are,

Ay amid all men bear himself thereafter
    Smit with a solemn and a sweet surprise,
Dumb to their scorn and turning on their laughter
    Only the dominance of earnest eyes?

This hath he done and shall we not adore him?
    This shall he do and can we still despair?
Come let us quickly fling ourselves before him,
    Cast at his feet the burthen of our care,

Flash from our eyes the glow of our thanksgiving,
    Glad and regretful, confident and calm,
Then thro' all life and what is after living
    Thrill to the tireless music of a psalm.

Yea thro' life, death, thro' sorrow and thro' sinning
    He shall suffice me, for He hath sufficed:
Christ is the end, for Christ was the beginning,
    Christ the beginning, for the end is Christ.

F. W. H. Myers

3

The Discipline of Peril

When you shall hear of wars and commotions,
do not be terrified; for these things must come to
pass first, but the end will not come immediately.
(Luke 21:9)

Our Lord talks so much about peril and disaster and we
deliberately shut our eyes and hearts and minds to it. Then
when these things come, if we think at all, we are at our
wits' end—we do not know what to make of them.

"These things have I told you, that when the time
comes, you may remember that I told you of them" (John
16:4).

This question is on the lips of people today: Is war of
the devil or of God? It is of neither. It is of humanity, though
God and the devil are both behind it. War is a conflict of
wills, either in individuals or in nations, and just now there
is a terrific conflict of wills in nations. If I cannot make my
will by diplomacy bear on other people, then the last resort
is war, and always will be until Jesus Christ brings in His
kingdom.

The Inevitability of Peril

War and commotions . . . must come to pass first.

Our Lord insists on the inevitability of peril. Right through His talks with His disciples, without panic and without passion and without fear, He says, "You must lay your account with this sort of thing, with war, with spite, with hatred, with jealousy, with despisings, with banishment, and with death. I have told you these things, that when they happen, you may remember that I told you of them, and not be scared."

Have we realized that the worst must happen? And yet Jesus says, "When you hear of wars and commotions do not be terrified." We are not only hearing of wars and commotions, they are here right enough. It is not imagination, it is not newspaper reports, the thing exists, there is no getting away from it.

Jesus Christ did not say, "You will understand why war has come," but "Do not be scared, do not be put in a panic." It is astonishing how we ignore what Jesus Christ tells us. He says that the nations will end in war and bloodshed and havoc; we ignore what He says, and when war does come we lose faith in God, we lose our wits and exhibit panic. The basis of panic is always cowardice.

The Impulse of Panic

Do not be terrified.

There is one thing worse than war, and that is sin. The thing that startles us is not the thing that startles God. We get tremendously scared when our social order is broken up, and well we may. We get terrorized by hundreds of people being killed, but we forget that there is something worse—sinful, dastardly lives being lived day by day, year in and year out, in our towns and cities—people without one trace of cleanness in their moral lives. That is worse.

How many of us in times of peace and civilization bother one iota about the state of people's hearts toward God? Yet these are the things that produce pain in the heart of God, not the wars and the devastation that so upset us. The human soul is so mysterious that in the moment of a great tragedy people get face-to-face with things they never gave heed to before, and in the moment of death it is extraordinary what takes place in the human heart toward God.

Are the terrors that are abroad producing panic—panic born of cowardice and selfishness? You never saw anybody in a panic who did not grab for themselves, whether it was sugar or butter or nations. Jesus would never allow His disciples to be in a panic. The one great crime on the part of a disciple, according to Jesus Christ, is worry. Whenever we begin to calculate without God we commit sin.

"Do not fret—it only causes harm" (Psalm 37:8).
Face facts. Very few of us will face facts. We prefer our fiction. Our Lord teaches us to look things full in the face and He says: "When you hear of wars and disturbances, do not be scared." It is the most natural thing in the world to be scared. There is no natural heart of man or woman that is not scared by these things, and the evidence that God's grace is at work amongst us is that we do not get terrified.

Our attitude must be: "Father, I do not know what these things mean: it looks like starvation and distress, but You have said, 'Do not be scared,' so I will not be; and You have said, 'Let not your heart be troubled,' so I will not let it be; and I stake my confidence in You." That is the real testimony.

It is very easy to trust in God when there is no difficulty, but that is not trust at all. It is simply letting the mind rest in a complacent mood. But when there is sickness in the house, when there is trouble, when there is death, where is our trust in God? The clearest evidence that God's grace is at work in our hearts is that we do not get into panics.

Christian Seemliness

> Take heed to yourselves . . . . Watch therefore, and pray always that you may be accounted worthy to escape all these things that will come to pass. (Luke 21:34, 36)

Seemliness is "conduct in accordance with the highest standard recognized." Our Lord in these verses describes the character of Christian conduct in the confusion at the end of this dispensation, that is, the day in which we live.

In verse 34, our Lord warns against the subtleties of indulgence. In verse 35, He describes the snare of war and confusion as inevitable, and in verse 36, He urges Christians to strenuously maintain their integrity.

Subtleties of Indulgence

> Take heed to yourselves, lest your hearts be weighed down with carousing, drunkenness, and cares of this life, and that Day come on you unex-pectedly. (Luke 21:34)

The most startling thing about this verse is that the Lord should have considered it necessary to warn Christians lest they sought distraction in these times of confusion by dissi-pation or drunkenness.

This verse is another indication of how our Lord will not allow Christians to build their conduct on suppositions based on ignorant innocence, but only on the revelation facts which He Himself gives. For instance, we should feel quite sure that we were not at all likely to seek distraction in these ways; but let us not forget that our Lord said, "Take heed to yourselves, lest . . . ."

Although our Lord talks of distraction in its final stages, we must remember that He condemns it in its initial stages. The beginning of carousing is indifference to present conditions from self-indulgence. We must take heed that in calamities, when war and devastation and heartbreak are abroad in the world, we do not shut ourselves up in a world of our own and ignore the demand made on us by our Lord and our fellowmen for the service of intercessory prayer and hospitality and care.

This same line of things holds good with regard to the dissipation of drunkenness and the cares of this life. The latter distraction to Christians is the most dangerous of all. A Christian must see to it that his interest in his possessions is not of such vital order that he is distracted from God.

Our Lord says that if these things are not heeded that Day will come upon us unexpectedly. If in that day any Christian finds himself in a panic, that is a sin which must be confessed and the burden of criminal carefulness laid at our Lord's feet, with a determination to follow a course more seemly according to God's standard for His saints.

Snare of the Inevitable

It will come as a snare on all those who dwell on the face of the whole earth. (Luke 21:35)

This verse states that the sudden arriving of this day of confusion will ensnare the whole world. It is not stated as a probability but as an inevitable certainty. Christians are counseled by our Lord to lay their account with the inevitable. Civilization and its amenities are made possible by Christianity, but they are not Christianity. It is these amenities which ensnare and devastate in the time in which we live and if we, by unspiritual self-indulgence have been living our lives in the externals, we shall be caught by this crisis and whirled into confusion.

There is a false sense of security produced by considering that there is safety in numbers. Our Lord in this verse states that the consternation will embrace "all those who dwell on the face of the whole earth," so that instead of numbers proving a security they prove an added element of terror. Have we taken heed and laid our account with these stern certainties, or are we as Christians indulging in the infatuation of any false security?

Strain of Integrity

> Watch therefore, and pray always that you may
> be accounted worthy to escape. (Luke 21:36)

The striking thing about these words is that the escape is not the free gift of God, but the result of Christian integrity. This verse is positive in its counsel as the other verses are positive in their commands. The counsel is to keep awake and pray. That our Lord should think fit to counsel prayer in time of conflict when practical common sense would place active doing first, reveals how totally different society's concepts are from our Lord's. Prayer seems suitable for old men and women and sentimental young people, but for all others it is apt to be looked upon as a religious weakness.

There are many things in the minds of Christians which are not yet brought into captivity to the obedience of Christ. Prayer is always answered rightly by God, our Lord says; no wonder we have to keep awake and pray, for thousands of people are being hurled into eternity during this time. Are we keeping awake and praying, or are we amazed at the magnitude of the slaughter? Countries are devastated, cities are sacked, commerce is tied up, hundreds are bankrupt, millions out of work, innumerable homes are blighted and broken; are we keeping awake and praying?

When the veil is lifted we shall find that the seemly conduct of prayer wrought the things of God in others. Let us keep awake and readjust ourselves to our Lord's counsel. He counsels His children to keep alert, to be pure, to yield to no temptation to panic, to false emotion, to illegitimate gain, or to a cowardly sense of futility. We can never be where we are not. We are just where we are. Let us keep alert and pray just there for His sake. Then our Lord says we shall be accounted worthy to escape all these things that shall come to pass, and to stand before the Son of Man—stand, not lie, nor grovel, nor cry, but stand upright, in the full integrity of Christian manhood and womanhood before the Son of Man.

The seemliness of Christian conduct is not consistent adherence to a mere principle of peace, but standing true to Jesus Christ. Let us stop all futile wailings that express themselves in such statements as "War ought not to be." War *is,* and we must not waste our time or our Lord's by giving way to any surfeit of screaming invective for or against anyone or anything. But "casting down arguments and every high thing that exalts itself against the knowledge of God" in connection with ourselves, let us face life as it is, not as we feel it ought to be, for it never will be what it ought to be until the kingdom of this world is become the kingdom of our Lord, and of His Christ.

Let us gird up the loins of our minds, watch and be sober, and behave in the seemly manner of those who look for their Lord.

Slighted Security

> If you had known . . . the things that make for your peace! But now they are hidden from your eyes . . . because you did not know the time of your visitation. (Luke 19:42–44)

The Burdened Sense

> From the end of the earth I will cry to You, when my heart is overwhelmed. (Psalm 61:2)

The feeling of bewilderment, of burden and perplexity is busy with the margins of many minds today; although the heart remains stout in its confidence in God, yet the senses are burdened with perplexity and misgiving. We shall be wise to let these things "lead us to the Rock that is higher" than we are.

Incredible things do happen.

"The kings of the earth, and all the inhabitants of the world, would not have believed that the adversary and the enemy could enter the gates of Jerusalem" (Lamentations 4:12).

That ancient peril is apt to repeat itself today, namely, a proud arrogance arising from intellectual confidence in God's prophetic Word, irrespective of the heart's condition. God has not any favorites outside faithfulness. God's order is the beginning and the end; His permissive will is the middle. God's eternal purposes will be fulfilled, but His permissive will allows Satan, sin, and strife to produce all kinds of misconceptions and false confidences until we all, individually as well as collectively, realize that His order is best. It is possible to build up a false security, as Israel and Judah did of old, based on God's own prophetic Word, but which ignores heart purity and humility before Him. The destruction of a certain class of prophetic student is stated by our Lord:

"Many will say to Me in that day, 'Lord, Lord, have we not prophesied in Your name . . . ?' And then will I declare to them, 'I never knew you' " (Matthew 7:22–23).

It was not that what they prophesied was not true, but it was not participated in by any whose hearts are regenerated by God's Spirit, no matter what their nationality may be. The ancient city of Jerusalem stands for all time as the symbol of destructive infatuation based on God's Word, whereas God's Word is only interpreted by the fulfilled in regenerated hearts and lives.

There is no road back to yesterday.

"He found no place for repentance, though he sought it diligently with tears" (Hebrews 12:17).

There are irreparable things. To God alone there is no irreparable past. We are delivered from sin by our Lord Jesus Christ, but He alone is the sinless One; we can never be as though we had not sinned. The gates of Paradise were irreparably closed to Adam and Eve and were never entered again by them (see Revelation 2:7). "The years that the locust has eaten" (see Joel 2:25) shall be restored, but only to a regenerated community.

What we need to heed in these days is that the unregenerate heart can never perceive the rule of God: "Unless one is born again, he cannot see the kingdom of God" (John 3:3). An unadjusted intellect, no matter if the heart be regenerated, will work itself untold destruction: "in which [in Paul's epistles] are some things hard to understand, which those who are untaught and unstable people twist to their own destruction, as they do also the rest of the Scriptures" (2 Peter 3:16).

We do well to insist carefully for ourselves on the fact that although the kingdom-revelation may be the key word to our Lord's teaching, the key word to the life to which alone that teaching applies is the Cross. The disciples were not told that by the interpretation of prophecy would all be drawn to God, but—"I, if I am lifted up from the earth, will draw all peoples to Myself" (John 12:32).

"When you lift up the Son of Man, then you will know that I am He, and that I do nothing of Myself; but as My Father taught me, I speak these things" (John 8:28).

The Bland Satisfaction

> If you had known, even you, especially in this your day. . . . (Luke 19:42)

The tears of the Redeemer over Jerusalem are without parallel for significance and teaching. Our Lord said to the daughters of Jerusalem, who were undergoing paroxysms of tears over Him:

"Daughters of Jerusalem, do not weep for Me, but weep for yourselves and for your children" (Luke 23:28).

The tears of our Lord embrace the divine knowledge of Jerusalem's irreparable past: "O Jerusalem, Jerusalem, the one who kills the prophets and stones those who are sent to her!" (Matthew 23:37); the divine knowledge of God's order: "I, John, saw the holy city, New Jerusalem, coming down out of heaven from God, prepared as a bride adorned for her husband" (Revelation 21:2); and the divine knowledge of God's permissive will: "How often I wanted to gather your children together, as a hen gathers her chicks under her wings, but you were not willing! See! Your house is left to you desolate" (Matthew 23:37–38).

It is too late now. The bland satisfaction, that smooth, mild infatuation which arises from pride and arrogance, has not only perverted her knowledge and her power of reading events, but given her a great sense of security. This is of great significance today.

If there is bland satisfaction in the conscience of any nation, then disillusionment and sudden destruction is certain. But are we quite free individually from this bland satisfaction? It is perilously possible to be fatally ignorant of our true relationship to things and to God, and for that ignorance to be culpable. Are we blandly satisfied that it is all right and yet we are not born from above? Are we still stiff-necked? Then sudden destruction comes. It is too late now to mourn over our indifference, but wake up, call on God and be saved!

The Belittled Security

. . . the things that make for your peace! (Luke 19:42)

Jerusalem and Jesus! What a contrast! With what an amazed stare of contempt the personal powers of Jerusalem confronted Jesus, the despised and rejected! Yet He was their peace for time and eternity, and the things that made for their peace were all connected with Him. He said to His disciples:

"These things I have spoken to you, that in Me you may have peace. In the world you will have tribulation; but be of good cheer, I have overcome the world" (John 16:33).

The parallels of belittled security may be many, but our aim here is more personal. Are we belittling our own security? It is easy to do it. Just as nations place their confidence for security in armaments or arbitration (as the whim takes them) and neglect the worship of God as the only security, so individuals may easily place confidence in the amenities of society, in civilized entrenchments, in a good home and a good situation, and belittle the one abiding security—*in God!*

To be indifferent to our Lord's claims is to belittle our security and remain in infatuation, out of which it will one day be too late to deliver us.

Rouse yourselves; it is too late now to mourn over the days and years in which you did not watch with your Lord, but wake up now!

The Blind Spot

> They are hidden from your eyes. . . . because you did not know the time of your visitation. (Luke 19:42, 44)

Like Nelson when he put the telescope to his blind eye that he might not see the order to retreat, so Jerusalem saw only in the direction of her prejudices. Here among them stood God Incarnate, a visitation from God Himself, but pride and arrogance and self-sufficiency blinded them and they saw Him not; they called Him "a glutton and a winebibber," they called Him "a sinner," "a Samaritan," they said that He was "out of His mind," and that He was demon-possessed. And this fatal blindness arose merely from not wanting to see certain things.

An immediate danger today is to apply all this to nations and to feel a sense of peculiar national security by noting the blind spot in another country's outlook. But our aim must be to see that we have no blind spot ourselves, no spot of obtuse obstinacy which has slowly formed itself into a blind spot in which we too cannot see the day of our visitation, the day in which God is visiting us. Nay, let us apply it personally—Have I a blind spot? Am I purposely, even judiciously, blind whenever I hear anyone testifying to deliverance from sin, or to the baptism of the Holy Spirit, or to the amazing positive things that happen when God is seen?

The Blessed Sense

> See! Your house is left to you desolate; for I say to you, you shall see Me no more till you say,

"Blessed is He who comes in the name of the Lord."
(Matthew 23:38–39)

It is too late to mourn in futile fashion over days of sin and pride and self-interest. Just as it is certain that desolation and havoc and misery will come in the wake of war, so it is certain that desolation and havoc are in your life because of sin. But what a day of rejoicing it will be when you say, "Blessed is He who comes in the name of the Lord!" Why not now, in a humbling sense of confessed sin, bow down under the mighty hand of God that where sin abounded, He may make grace much more abound. God hasten the day when "the kingdom of this world is become the kingdom of our Lord, and of His Christ."

Fitness

I have been crucified with Christ; it is no longer I who live, but Christ lives in me; and the life which I now live in the flesh I live by faith in the Son of God, who loved me and gave Himself for me.
(Galatians 2:20)

There are three things in this verse about personal fitness for what the Lord requires of us, all full of pressing personal importance.

The Relinquished Life—"I have been crucified with Christ."

The Distinguished Life—"It is no longer I who live, but Christ lives in me."

The Extinguished Life—"The life which I now live in the flesh I live by faith in the Son of God, who loved me and gave Himself for me."

These are three aspects of the one great theme of personal identification with our Lord.

I have been crucified with Christ.

No one is ever united with the Lord Jesus Christ until he is willing to relinquish all of the life he held before. This does not only mean relinquishing sin, it means relinquishing the whole way of looking at things. To be born from above of the Spirit of God means that we must let go before we lay hold.

There are many people who believe in Jesus Christ but they have not relinquished anything, consequently they have not received anything; there is still the realization of a life that has not been relinquished, and this great word of the apostle Paul's is a foreign language altogether. It is not practical to them, it is "in the clouds," literally there is "nothing in it." But, blessed be the name of God, there *is* something in it!

In the first stages it is a relinquishing of pretense. What our Lord Jesus Christ wants us to present to Him is not our goodness, or our honesty, or our endeavor, but our real solid sin. That is all He can take. "He made Him who knew no sin to be sin for us." And what does He give in exchange for our solid sin? Great solid righteousness—"that we might become the righteousness of God in Him"—but we must relinquish all pretense of being anything. We must relinquish in every way all claim to being worthy of God's consideration. That is the meaning of conviction of sin.

A word to those who have been quickened by the Spirit of God and introduced into His kingdom—they have had their eyes opened and know something of what our Lord said to Nicodemus, "Unless one is born again, he cannot see the kingdom of God" (John 3:3). If we can say, "I have been quickened by the Spirit and I do perceive the rule of God," then in us the Spirit of God will show what further there is to relinquish. There must be the relinquishing of my right to myself in every phase and condition of it. Am I willing to relinquish my hold on my life, my hold on all I possess, my hold on all my affections, my hold on everything? Am I willing to be God's child, and to be so identified with the death of the Lord Jesus Christ that I too know I have been crucified with Him?

There may be a sharp, painful disillusionment to go through before we do relinquish. When a person really sees himself as the Lord Jesus Christ sees him, it is not the abominable social sins of the flesh that shock him, it is the awful nature of the pride of his own heart against the Lord Jesus Christ—the shame, the horror, the desperate conviction that comes when we realize ourselves in the light of Jesus Christ as the Spirit of God reveals Him to us. That is the true gift of repentance and the real meaning of it.

Are you hoodwinking your own soul by an intellectual comprehension of God's prophetic truth while you are perfectly unfit in moral life, in spiritual life, and in domestic life, to meet Him? God grant that today the Spirit of God may come to you and to me and make us know whether we are living this relinquished life.

If we are going to fly, things that would prevent must not have any hold on us. Lusts of the flesh, desires of the mind, possessions, must all go. One thing we are realizing today is that to the majority of us civilized life is an elaborate way of doing without God. We have not been living life hid with Christ in God; we have been living in the abundance of the things which we possess. When they are shaken, terror, panic, and mental imbecility have laid hold of people who are normally very strong-minded and disdainful with regard to the phase of truth, but the shattering of the pillars of their refuge has come. Thank God, He still leaves His mighty, winning, wooing Spirit with us. "I have been crucified with Christ"—it is a real, definite personal experience.

The Distinguished Life: Fitness to Fight

It is no longer I who live, but Christ lives in me.

This life has marked characteristics entirely of its own. Paul is stating that the relinquished life has found him identified with his Lord, and now all the great power of God is distinguishing him as a different person from the one he was before. He does not hate what he used to hate. He used to persecute and despise the followers of Jesus Christ; he despises them no longer. Not only does he not despise them, but he is identified with them and with their Lord. After Pentecost we read that "they realized that they had been with Jesus." They saw the strong, distinguished family likeness in them and recognized it at once as the Lord Jesus Christ.

One great characteristic in the life of a person whose life is hid with Christ in God is that he has received the gift Jesus Christ gives. What gift does Jesus Christ give to those who are identified with Him? The gift His Father gave Him, the Father gave Him the Cross, and He gives us our cross: "If anyone desires to come after Me, let him deny himself, and take up his cross, and follow Me" (Matthew 16:24). Let him relinquish, give up his right to himself—distinguished by one thing, "Do you not know . . . you are not your own? For you were bought at a price" (1 Corinthians 6:19–20). To take up our cross daily means that we take now what otherwise would go to Jesus Christ. The distinguished life means that we fill up in our flesh "what is lacking in the afflictions of Christ for the sake of His body, which is the church." That means the practical fulfillment of Matthew 11:29, "Take My yoke upon you and learn from Me, for I am gentle and lowly in heart." There is nothing to fill up of that which remains lacking in His sufferings for His body's sake. Are we distinguished as the ones in whom Christ lives, meeting things as He did? If so, we are fit for flying, for fighting, and for following.

The Extinguished Life: Fitness for Following

> The life which I now live in the flesh I live by faith in the Son of God, who loved me and gave Himself for me.

There is no more of the old disposition manifested in this man, Paul the apostle. There is no "Saul of Tarsus" disposition manifested; that has been extinguished—it has died right out! This is much more than sin, mark you, it is all the old way of reasoning; what is manifested now, Paul says, is faith in the Son of God. Do you remember what this man said: "When it pleased God, who separated me from my mother's womb and called me through His grace, to reveal His Son in me . . ." (Galatians 1:15-16)? The characteristic that is manifested is faith in the Son of God, the Lord Jesus Christ, seeing the full purpose and meaning of His own life working through the apostle Paul.

Is that altogether beside the mark? It is the practical clear direct message of God to your heart and mine today—a perfect fitness by the wonderful redemption of our Lord Jesus Christ being realized in us as we relinquish.

You will find the supreme crises in your life are Will issues all the time. *Will* I relinquish? *Will* I abandon? It is not that God won't make us fit, it is that He cannot. God cannot make us fit to meet Him in the air unless we are willing to let Him. He cannot make us fit as the dwellings of His Son unless we are willing, because He wants sons and daughters. If you are up against a crisis, go through with it, relinquish all, and let Him make you fit for all He requires of you in this day.

First And Last

I am the way, the truth, and the life. No one comes to the Father except through Me. (John 14:6)

The words of our Lord come to one as those that alone can be welcomed on the threshold of each new year. Other people's words are too fraught with personal prejudice or clouded by personal pain to convey a message for this New Year. There are thousands of hearts and minds too distracted by this terrible war to receive with meekness any other words than those of our Lord Jesus Christ.

The Way

I am the way.

Thomas' depressed exclamation, "Lord, we do not know where You are going, and how can we know the way?" is the language of many a heart today, and if all the saints and all the suffering and sorrowing ones would only listen to our Lord's reply, we would all be strong to bear, and rejoicing to do in the strength of the Lord.

Our Lord said, "I am the way," not the way to anyone or anything; He is not a road we leave behind us, He is the way to the Father in whom we abide (see John 15:4). He *is* the way, not, He *was* the way, and there is not any way of living in the fatherhood of God except by living in Christ. Whoever finds himself in Christ finds life (see Proverbs 8:35). The way to the Father is not by the law, nor by obedience, or creed, but Jesus Christ Himself. He is the way of the Father whereby any and every soul may be in peace, in joy, and in divine courage during the days of this coming year. In any assailing tribulation our Lord says, "that in Me you may have peace." When imagination brooding on wars and rumors of wars is apt to frighten the souls of men and women, Christ Jesus is the way of the fatherhood of God, sustaining, and comforting, and joyous.

To all those who are in the way let me urge you by abiding in Jesus to let the rivers of living water pour through you to heal the brokenhearted, to set at liberty the oppressed, and to proclaim the acceptable year of the Lord.

The Truth

I am . . . the truth.

Amid all the whirling contentions and confusion produced in people's minds by what is called truth, again our Lord's word to Thomas abides, "I am the truth." Truth is not a system, not a constitution, nor even a creed; the truth is the Lord Jesus Christ Himself, and He is the truth about the Father just as He is the way of the Father. Our tendency is to make truth a logical statement, to make it a principle instead of a person. Profoundly speaking, there are no Christian principles, but the saint by abiding in Christ in the way of the fatherhood of God discerns the truth of God in the passing moments. Confusion arises when we disassociate ourselves from our Lord and try to live up to a standard merely constructed on His Word.

In John 14:8–11, our Lord distinctly says that He and the Father are one. Would that those who name the name of Christ realized that He *is* the truth, not the proclaimer of it; that He *is* the gospel, not the preacher of the gospel; that He *is* the way of the fatherhood of God. What men and women need is the "fathering" of God, so that from all fright and fear they may be held steady by the gentleness of God, and that is only realized in Christ. Those of us who do know it have a gracious ministry to maintain, so abiding in Him that we reveal the truth as it is in Jesus in our going in and out among the devastated and distracted.

The Life

> I am . . . the life.

Many start this year from weariness of life crying to God that they might die. The light of their eyes has been taken from them, the prospects of life have been extinguished and all they held most dear has been shattered in no sentimental way but in a very real sense. Again the superb declaration of our Lord, "I am the life," comes with eternal succor. He is the life of the Father just as He is the Father's way and the Father's truth. "The gift *of* God is eternal life"; not the gift *from* God, as if eternal life were a present given by God: it is Himself. The life imparted by our Lord is the life of God, and the sacrament of the Lord's Supper is the visible commemoration of this ever-abiding fact. "For as often as you eat this bread and drink this cup, you proclaim the Lord's death till He comes" (1 Corinthians 11:26).

Let us remember that Jesus Christ is life, and our life, (all our fresh springs are in Him) so that whether we eat or drink, or whatever we do, let us do all to the glory of God. May this be a year in which those of us who are God's children manifest the life of God in our mortal flesh.

We are near the end of the present order, and the throes and weariness of exhausted turmoil are concentrated in many hearts and lives. What is needed is the life of the Father which is ours in Jesus Christ. He said, "I have come that they may have life" (John 10:10); and He also said, "You are not willing to come to Me that you may have life" (John 5:40). Let those of us who are God's children be the conductors of the life of God to exhausted men and women till they, too, are made one with Him.

The Exclusive One

> No one comes to the Father except through Me.

Many today are realizing the futility of beautiful sentimental phrases about the fatherhood of God; they are finding them beautiful untruths. The words of our Lord, "no one comes to the Father except through Me," reveal the error and at the same time open the way to the Father. Our Lord Jesus Christ is the exclusive way to the Father. By His Cross alone one enters into the adoption of a child of God. Our Lord did not say, "No one comes to *God* except through Me." There are many ways of coming to God other than by the Lord Jesus Christ, but no one ever came to the *Father* except through Jesus Christ. He is the exclusive way there, the constant active medium to our intercourse with the Father.

This war, which for a time has made those in pain say petulant, unbelieving things about the creeds that are right in theory but utterly futile in practice, has at the same time prepared their hearts for the universality of the exclusive way of Christ to the Father. He is the only way to the Father, but it is a way that is open to anyone and everyone, the way that knows "neither Greek nor Jew, . . . barbarian, Scythian, slave nor free, but Christ is all and in all." It is the duty and privilege of those who are Christ's to proclaim this glorious revelation with lip and life, with impassioned zeal and earnestness in the closing phases of the dispensation in which we live.

God grant that this year may find each one of us abiding in the way, incorporated into the truth, infused by the life, and manifesting the mighty Fatherhood of God in and through our Lord Jesus Christ. In the name that is above every name we pray that this year may be the year of the first and the last, the beginning and the end, our Lord Jesus Christ.

God's Parenthesis

Yes, a sword will pierce through your own soul also. (Luke 2:35)

A parenthesis is a phrase or sentence inserted in another which is grammatically complete without it, and if you want to understand the author, pay particular attention to the parenthesis.

God puts a parenthesis in the middle flow of our lives—if you want to understand your life, read the parenthesis if you can. There was a parenthesis in Hezekiah's life and when he was through it, he said, "I shall go as in a solemn procession all my years." A short time after, though, he forgot and began to knuckle under and compromise with a pagan king.

Have we been paying sufficient attention to the parentheses God puts in our lives? It may have been good fortune, it may have been bad fortune, it may have been a delightful friendship, it may have been a heartbreak. But when God sums up our lives, it is the parentheses which really give the heart of our lives with Him.

Impaired by God

> The Holy Spirit will come upon you, and the power of the Highest will overshadow you; therefore, also, that Holy One who is to be born will be called the Son of God. (Luke 1:35)

The Virgin Mary is not only unique as the mother of our Lord, but she stands as the type of what we must expect if we are going to be those whom our Lord calls "My brother and sister and mother" (Matthew 12:50). Simeon was completely possessed, guided, and controlled by the Holy Spirit, and when he saw Mary he spoke these wonderful words:

"Behold, this Child is destined for the fall and rising of many in Israel . . . (Yes, a sword will pierce through your own soul also), that the thoughts of many hearts may be revealed" (Luke 2:34–35).

When Christ is formed in us by the power of regeneration, our natural lives experience exactly the same thing, that is, a sword that we would never have had if we were not born again of God, a type of suffering that we would know nothing about if the Son of God were not formed in us.

When the angel saluted her, Mary was amazed and staggered. After the Holy Spirit had come upon her, her life was impaired, full of embarrassment and terror. It is an abiding truth that when we are born of the Holy Spirit, instantly the life becomes impaired from every merely natural standpoint.

When we receive God's Spirit, God suddenly opens up His purpose for our lives. Then when the "angel" departs we begin to realize exactly what an impaired life means if we go on with it. It means that each life will produce one or two characteristics people will sneer at, one or two characteristics people will be contemptuous over, thoroughly annoyed and angry over. It was so with Mary. The sword Simeon spoke of very soon began to pierce through her own soul.

We need to remind ourselves of the stern, heroic stuff Jesus Christ always spoke when He talked about discipleship. "If anyone desires to come after Me, let him deny himself, and take up his cross daily, and follow Me" (Luke 9:23). Few of us do it though plenty of us talk about it. It means an impaired life. "A sword will pierce through your own soul also."

You have been full of complaints these past months and have blamed everything but yourself; the reason is you were not prepared for an impaired life as far as this world was concerned. The beginnings of God's life in a man or woman are directly across the will of nature, because nature has to be transformed in your particular bodily life and mine into a spiritual life by obedience. Obedience to the Spirit of God means a maimed life, maimed in a hundred and one ways, and in the closest relationships of all (see Luke 14:26).

The Impeded Life with God

> Woman, what does your concern have to do with Me? (John 2:4)

This new life impedes us in our natural outlook and ways until we get these rightly related by having "put on the new man," until the Son of God is formed in us and both the natural and the holy are the same.

The natural in us wants the Son of God to do Almighty God's work in *our* way. What could be better than that the Son of God should manifest the fact that He is in us? Thousands saved in a day! Ourselves transformed and held as marvelous specimens of what God can do! Something wonderful performed at the dictates of our natural (not sinful) lives! We want Him to do this and that, we demand He should do it, we rush in and say, "Now this is the time," but we receive a real check from God which means that we dare not open our mouths to Him again on the subject. When our Lord's miracles are at work in us they always manifest themselves in a chastened life, utterly restrained.

Has God's parenthesis come to you by impeding some great natural impulse? You are a child of God. You started off to work for Him and expected Him to do wonderful things. In fact you demanded He should do them; then He brought you into a corner and you were rebuked directly by the Son of God.

Is that the parenthesis God has put in your life just now? Some purpose, some aim of yours in God's work that you were expecting Him to manifest immediately by a mighty miracle, but instead there came the extinction of your naturally good impulse. Nobody heard the rebuke but you, but when the miracle was wrought you were able to understand and to listen to Him. Beware of listening to your own point of view when the Son of God has come.

The Insulated Life with God

Now there stood by the cross of Jesus His mother. (John 19:25)

To insulate means "to place in a detached position." The sword began to pierce very early in Mary's life, and it pierced all through. Now she stands at the cross with her own Son, in whom every Scripture and oracle of God has centered. He has been through His agony and His mother could do nothing for Him. She could not understand the depth of the agony of Gethsemane; now she sees Him on the cross and what happens? Jesus sees her and says, "Woman, behold your son!" and to John, "Behold your mother!" That is an illustration of what happens when the life of the Son of God and the full purpose of God are being worked out in us in ways we cannot understand but do not doubt.

Beware of saying, "I do not need any discipline. I am saved and sanctified, therefore, everything I think is right." Nothing we think is right—only what God thinks in us is right. The Son of God revealed exactly how a person's brain and body and will were to be used if he was to live in obedience to God. Our Lord submitted His intelligence to His Father, and He submitted His will to His Father. "I came not to do My own will," He says over and over again.

There are great perplexities in life, but thank God, if we will trust with the bold, implicit trust of our natural life, in the Son of God, He will bring out His perfect, complete purposes in and through our particular lives.

Are You Ever Disturbed?

> Peace I leave with you, My peace I give to you;
> not as the world gives, do I give to you. Let not your
> heart be troubled, neither let it be afraid. (John 14:27)

Have You Ever Received in This Way?

The disciples, like many today, were not in a state to provide their own inner peace. There are times when inner peace is based on ignorance. But when we awake to the troubles of life, which more than ever before surge and heave in threatening billows, inner peace is impossible unless it is received from our Lord. When our Lord spoke peace, He made peace. His words are ever spirit and life. Have you ever received what He spoke?

The peace of sins forgiven, the peace of a conscience at rest with God, is not the peace that Jesus imparts. Those are the immediate results of believing and obeying Him, but it is His own peace He gives, and He never had any sins to be forgiven or an outraged conscience to appease. Have you ever received His peace? When you are right with God, receive your peace by studying in consecrated concentration our Lord Himself. It is the peace that comes from looking at His face and remembering the undisturbed condition of our Lord in every set of circumstances. "But we all, with unveiled face, beholding as in a mirror the glory of the Lord, are being transformed into the same image from glory to glory" (2 Corinthians 3:18).

Are you painfully disturbed just now, distracted by the waves and billows of God's providential permission, and having turned over, as it were, the boulders of your belief, you still find no well of peace or joy or comfort—all is barren? Then look up and receive the undisturbed peace of our Lord Jesus Christ. Above and in the facts of war and pain and difficulties He reigns, peaceful. Reflected peace is the greatest evidence that I am right with God, for I am at liberty to turn my mind to Him. If I am not right with God I can never turn my mind anywhere but on myself. "Then I will go . . . to God my exceeding joy " (Psalm 43:4). Am I certain that God is not miserable? Then His joy will be my strength. We are changed by looking, not by introspection. The source of peace is God, not myself. It never is *my* peace but always *His,* and if He withdraws, it is not there. If I allow anything to hide the face, the countenance, the memory, the consideration of our Lord Jesus from me, then I am either disturbed or I have a false security. "Consider Him . . . lest you become weary and discouraged in your souls" (Hebrews 12:3). Nothing else is in the least like His peace. It is the peace of God which passes all understanding. Are you looking to Jesus just now in the immediate pressing matter and receiving from Him peace? Then He will be a gracious benediction of peace in and through you.

Have You Ever Recognized in This Way?

The world means what it says, but it cannot impart. Our Lord imparts what He says—He does not give like the world does. Will I be absolutely confident in Jesus? What does it matter what happens to me? The thought ought never to bother us. The thing that ought to occupy us is setting the Lord always before us (see Acts 20:24). Jesus Christ imparts the Holy Spirit to me, and the Holy Spirit sheds abroad the love of God in my heart. The peace of Jesus is not a cherished piece of property that I possess; it is a direct impartation from Him, and my enjoying His peace depends on my recognizing this.

This kind of peace banishes trouble just now and presently. Our Lord says in effect, "Don't let your heart be troubled out of its relationship with Me." It is never the big things that disturb us, but the trivial things. Do I believe that in the circumstances that are apt to bother me just now Jesus Christ is not perplexed at all? If I do, His peace is mine. If I try to worry it out, I obliterate Him and deserve what I get.

When we confer with Jesus Christ over other lives all the perplexity goes because He has no perplexity, and our concern is to abide in Him. The reason we get disturbed is that we have not been considering Him. Lay it all out before Him, and in the face of difficulties, bereavement and sorrow, hear Him say, "Let not your heart be troubled." Let us be confident in His wisdom and His certainty that all will be well. "He remains faithful; He cannot deny Himself" (2 Timothy 2:13). The angels' song is still the truth: "Glory to God in high heaven, and peace on earth for men whom He favors."

Radiant in the Thick of It

Who shall bring a charge against God's elect? It is God who justifies. Who is he who condemns? It is Christ who died, and furthermore is also risen, who is even at the right hand of God, who also makes intercession for us. Who shall separate us from the love of Christ? Shall tribulation, or distress, or perse-cution, or famine, or nakedness, or peril, or sword? As it is written, "For Your sake we are killed all day long; we are accounted as sheep for the slaughter." Yet in all these things we are more than conquerors through Him who loved us. For I am persuaded that neither death nor life, nor angels nor principalities nor powers, nor things present nor things to come, nor height nor depth, nor any other created thing, shall be able to separate us from the love of God which is in Christ Jesus our Lord. (Romans 8:33–39)

The Vocation of the Saint

They looked to Him and were radiant. (Psalm 34:5)

There are circumstances and difficulties which can only be described as "the thick of it," and in and through all such the apostle Paul says we are to be "more than conquerors." Paul always talked from the deep center of things, and the majority of us do not pay much attention to him until some calamity or disaster strikes us out of the shallows; then the Bible takes on a new guise and we find that it always speaks profoundly.

The vocation of a saint is to be in the thick of it "for Your sake." Whenever Jesus Christ refers to discipleship or to suffering, it is always, "for My sake." The deep relationship of a saint is a personal one and the reason a saint can be radiant is that he has lost interest in his own individuality and has become absolutely devoted to the person of the Lord Jesus Christ.

"Who shall bring a charge against God's elect? It is God who justifies" (Romans 8:33). When a saint puts his or her confidence in the election of God, no tribulation or affliction can ever touch that confidence. When we realize that there is no hope of deliverance in human wisdom, or in human rectitude, or in anything that we can do, then Paul counsels us to accept the justification of God and to stand true to the election of God in Christ Jesus. This is the finest cure for spiritual degeneration or for spiritual sulks.

"Who is he who condemns? It is Christ who died" (verse 34). "Christ died for the ungodly." Then is it a remarkable thing that after we have accepted His salvation we begin to find out our unworthiness? "Who is he who condemns? It is Christ who died." Stake your confidence in

Him! Let there be a real shifting of the whole center of life into confidence in Jesus Christ.

"Who shall separate us from the love of Christ?" (verse 35). In the confusion and turmoil of things, there is very little we can explain; things happen which upset all our calculations, but: "Who shall separate us from the love of Christ?" Nothing! When we know that nothing can separate us from the love of Christ, it does not matter what calamities may occur, we are as unshakable as God's throne.

The Valley of the Shadow

Yea, though I walk through the valley of the shadow of death, I will fear no evil. (Psalm 23:4)

"Who shall separate us from the love of Christ? Shall tribulation, or distress, or persecution, or famine?" Can we remain true to the vocation of the saint in tribulation? Think of the thousands who have had to go through tribulation during these past years—every human hope taken from them; yet the saint with an amazing hopefulness remains radiant in the thick of it.

"Or nakedness, or peril, or sword?" In our own day all these things are dastardly realities. Can we maintain our vocation as saints there? Life was going on all right when suddenly we were struck by a psychological nor'wester! Paul says we have to maintain our vocation in the midst of the most desperate things that can happen in individual life.

The Vision of Slaughter

For Your sake we are killed all day long; we are accounted as sheep for the slaughter. (Romans 8:36)

Everyone who comes to Jesus Christ has to go through the ordeal of condemnation. He has to have his beauty "melt away like a moth," and his righteousness drop from him "like filthy rags" when he stands face-to-face with God. "I am persuaded that neither death nor life, nor angels nor principalities"—these are things beyond our control, and they introduce painful agonies into our experience, they slaughter our hopes. "Nor things present"—things present prevail, things we cannot alter. A bereavement profoundly alters life, so does a joy, or a war: "nor things to come"—think of the number of bridges we have all crossed before we came to them! Things to come are always prevailing, human wisdom cannot touch them. "Nor powers," there are terrific powers that move around in total disregard of us. "Nor height nor depth, nor any other created thing." Can we maintain our vocation in the face of every terror? Paul says we can, because he is persuaded that none of these things "shall be able to separate us from the love of God which is in Christ Jesus our Lord."

It all comes back to this—am I radiant in the thick of it for His sake?

4

The Discipline of Prayer

The following quotation will suggest the right background for this introduction:

In the East the following phenomenon is often observed. Where the desert touches a river valley or oasis, the sand is in a continual state of drift from the wind, and it is this drift which is the real cause of the barrenness of such portions of the desert at least as abut upon the fertile land. For under the rain, or by infiltration of the river, plants often spring through the sand, and there is sometimes promise of considerable fertility. It never lasts. Down comes the periodic drift, and life is stunted or choked out. But set down a rock on the sand, and see the difference it makes. After a few showers, to the leeward side of this some blades will spring up; if you have patience, you will see in time a garden. How has the boulder produced this? Simply by arresting the drift.

George Adam Smith

A man will be as a hiding place from the wind, and a cover from the tempest, as rivers of water in a dry place, as the shadow of a great rock in a weary land. (Isaiah 32:2)

Our Lord Jesus Christ is just that rock to God's children.

He personally stays the drift of arduous Christian activities, of insidious mental skepticism, of intuitive uncertainties, and produces a sanctuary within which abide perennial inspiration and wonderful ways to imitate.

How many cease from praying by indiscernible, unconscious ways! They are not those who because of intellectual barriers have determined on prayerlessness or who have abandoned praying in favor of a cherished sin, but those who have ceased praying by more indecipherable ways.

The life of God in us is manifested by spiritual concentration, not by pious self-consciousness; pious self-consciousness produces the worship of prayer, which is anti-Christian. This unscriptural piety fixes itself on the actual incidents in such verses as Mark 1:35: "In the morning, having risen a long while before daylight, He went out and departed to a solitary place; and there He prayed." It disproportionately emphasizes "having risen a long while before daylight," implying that if this actual early rising were imitated it would produce Christlikeness in us; whereas our Lord prayed because He was concentrated on God. That is, He did not worship prayer.

There are sure to be resurgent, periodic drifts of skepticism destructive of all such unrobust, pious sentimentality, because the worshipping of prayer is not of the nature of reality. Spiritual effects are thus construed into spiritual causes, as if a "gift of prayer" were the cause of Christlikeness. It may be the cause of devotion, but it is the gift *from* prayer that matters, and this is the outcome of Christian concentration.

The intellectual desire to explain and thereby command is part of our natural inheritance, but it will turn into a tyrannical dictator if not kept strictly in its place as an instrument of the life and not the life itself; this can only be done by obedience (see Romans 12:2). The intellectual desire to dominate by explanation has so largely prevailed that prayer has become a mere borderland exercise of natural intelligence, wherein it is explained that prayer is the "reflex action" of a particular individual with the "God of all."

It is absurd to imagine anyone trying to think how they will live before they are born, yet it is this absurdity which the intellect tries to perform in connection with prayer. If the dominion of intellectual explanation is the characteristic of a naturally cultured life, dominion by obedience is the characteristic of the spiritually disciplined life. Intellectual expression in life is the effect of a naturally educated life, but is not the cause of the life; and the Christian experience of prayer is not its own cause, but the effect of the life of God in me. Prayer is the instrument of the life of worship, it is not worship itself. Intellect and prayer are united in the saint in the consciousness of Christ which we share. Consequently, the consciousness of self-realization is a perversion and a snare. Our spiritual certainty in prayer is God's divine certainty, not a side-eddy of sanctimoniousness.

> O patient, patient God,
> Misprized, profaned God,
> Grieved and wounded God,

Dooming and quickening God,
We weary of the victim faint,
The hero martyr, peasant saint,
Who stirs our love but leaves our taint,
Is balm but never rod,
Nor rends our last green sod,
Or tombs restraint.
We crave the Eternal Holy Son,
Earth's Lord and hell's, the Living One,
Straight from His cross, His grave, His throne,
With a world-pardon all our own;
With sacramental imminence
Transcending our abased sense;
With eyes of flame at which we fall
Dead men, till He our life recall,
And be our life, our all in all.
With all the church's faithful folk,
This Lord, this Spirit, we invoke.

In order to present this study on the "Discipline of Prayer" in as direct a way as possible, it is put under headings.

The Position of Prayer

When you pray, you must not be like the hypocrites, for they like to stand and pray in the synagogues and at the street corners, so as to be seen by men; I tell you truly, they do get their reward. When you pray, go into your room and shut the door, pray to your Father who is in secret, and your Father who sees what is secret will reward you. Do not pray by idle rote like pagans, for they suppose they will be heard the more they say; you must not copy them; your Father knows your needs before you ask him. (Matthew 6:5–9, MOFFAT)

This general heading indicates that it is important to notice that in the New Testament, and in the life of our Lord, prayer is not so much an acquired culture as the implicit nature of the spiritual life itself. Outside the New Testament prayer is apt to be presented as something entirely acquired, something placed in the position of a meritorious decoration for valiant service in piety. In other words, the position we are apt to give to prayer is too consciously an attainment of communion, and thus it is presented out of all proportion, so that in times of spiritual decline we are inclined to place in the forefront the need of prayer instead of a penitent approach to God.

> Yet Thou art oft most present, Lord,
>   In weak distracted prayer;
> A sinner out of heart with self
>   Most often finds Thee there.
>
> For prayer that humbles, sets the soul
>   From all illusions free,
> And teaches it how utterly,
>   Dear Lord, it hangs on Thee.

The Place of Prayer

Pray without ceasing. (1 Thessalonians 5:17)

There is a quietism of devotional self-indulgence which takes the place spiritually that loafing does socially. It is easy to call it meditative prayer, but meditation is only attained in actual life by the strenuous discipline of brooding in the center of a subject. God gives of His abundant grace and the divine fire of instinctive inspiration, but we must acquire the technical skill of expressing that genius of God in our lives. There are spiritual loafers who are painfully impressionable about "tones" and "moods" and "places," and they remind one of the aesthetic affectation of many persons who have not enough of the artist in them to work arduously and overcome technical difficulties, so they live lives of self-indulgent sentimental artistic indolence. An artist is never consciously artistic, and a saint is never consciously a praying one. A saint endeavors consciously and strenuously to master the technical means of expressing God's life in himself. The place of prayer in the New Testament is just this one of severe technical training in which spiritual sympathies are sustained in unsecular strength and manifested in the vulgar details of actual life.

The Platform of Prayer

> Therefore brethren, having boldness to enter the Holiest by the blood of Jesus . . . . (Hebrews 10:19)

Prayer does not bring us into contact with the rationality of human existence but into accordance with eternal reality. The great reality is redemption, and redemption is the platform of prayer. The historic fact of the death of Jesus is redemptive reality brought to us as a fact which creates belief in itself. Let Hebrews 10:19 be realized, and many pietistic perils of the devotional life will never appear again. Reality is not in intellect or intuitions, but in the conscience reacting to redemption through the whole nature. We are based on the platform of reality in prayer by the atonement of our Lord Jesus Christ. It is not our earnestness that brings us into touch with God, nor our devotion, nor our times of prayer, but our Lord Jesus Christ's vitalizing death. Our times of prayer are evidences of reaction on the reality of redemption, so we have confidence and boldness of access into the holiest. What an unspeakable joy it is to know that we each have the right of approach to God in confidence, that the place of the ark is our place, "Therefore, brethren, having boldness." What an awe and what a wonder of privilege, "to enter the Holiest," in the perfection of the atonement, "by the blood of Jesus."

The Purpose of Prayer

> Be anxious for nothing, but in everything by prayer and supplication, with thanksgiving, let your requests be made known to God. (Philippians 4:6)

To forebode is to forbid communion with God. The child of God can never think of anything the heavenly Father will forget; then to worry is spiritual irritability with our Lord. Prayer is the evidence that I am spiritually concentrated on God, when to forethink is but to pray about everything, and to live in actual conditions is to be thankful in anything. Prayer is not to be used as the petted privilege of a spoiled child seeking for ideal conditions in which to indulge his spiritual propensities ad lib—the purpose of prayer is the maintenance of fitness in an ideal relationship with God amid conditions which ought not to be merely ideal but really actual. Actualities are not here to be idealized, but to be realized, while by prayer we lay hold on God and He unites us into His consciousness. The purpose of prayer is to reveal the presence of God equally present all the time in every condition.

> For perfect childlike confidence in Thee;
> For childlike glimpses of the life to be;
> For trust akin to my child's trust in me;
> For hearts at rest through confidence in Thee;

For hearts triumphant in perpetual hope;
For hope victorious through past hopes fulfilled;
For mightier hopes born of the things we know;
For faith born of the things we may not know;
For hope of powers increased ten thousand fold;
For that last hope of likeness to Thyself,
When hope shall end in glorious certainty;
>   *With quickened hearts*
>   That find Thee everywhere,
>   We thank Thee, Lord!

The Particulars of Prayer

It is of the greatest importance to think of prayer as our Lord taught in regard to it. Our Lord never referred to unanswered prayer. He taught that prayers are *always* answered, "Everyone who asks receives" (Luke 11:10). He ever implied that prayers are answered rightly because of the heavenly Father's wisdom, "Your Father knows the things you have need of before you ask Him" (Matthew 6:8). In regard to prayer, we are apt to be apologetic and apathetic, complex and confused; yet what a splendid audacity a childlike child has! And that is what our Lord taught us to have.

"I thank You, Father, Lord of heaven and earth, that You have hidden these things from the wise and prudent and have revealed them to babes" (Matthew 11:25).

"Assuredly, I say to you, unless you are converted and become as little children, you will by no means enter the kingdom of heaven" (Matthew 18:3).

We may be converted, but obviously we have too often *not* become as little children.

Our Motive

> When you pray, you shall not be like the hyp-
> ocrites. For they love to pray standing in the syna-
> gogues and on the corners of the streets, that they
> may be seen by men. Assuredly, I say to you, they
> have their reward. (Matthew 6:5)

Surely there is a great glow of humor in our Lord's
words, "Assuredly, I say to you, they have their reward," as
one who should say, "That is all there is to it." Their motive
is to be seen of men; they are seen of men, and that is their
reward, placarded "pi-ness!" Watch your motive; is it a
pose arising from a real enchantment? (The word hypocrites here is really "playactors.") You very earnestly and
solemnly tax your resources to be a praying person; people
call at your house but cannot see you because it is your
time for prayer. You perhaps have not noticed before that
you always take care to tell those to whom it matters how
early you rise in the morning to pray, how many all nights
of prayer you spend, and you have great zealousness in pro-
claiming your protracted meetings. This is all pious playacting. Jesus says, "Don't do it." Our Lord did not say it was
wrong to pray at the corners of the street, but He did say it
was wrong to have the motive to be *seen of men*. It is not
wrong to pray in the early morning, but it is wrong to have
the motive that it should be known. Avoid every tendency
away from the simplicity of relationship to God in Christ
Jesus, and then prayer will be as the breath of the lungs in a
healthy body. It is at first difficult to learn a new and better
way of breathing, consequently we are conscious of it for a
time, but it is merely consciousness of what will by habit
become an unconscious possession. So in the better and
new way of breathing spiritually in prayer, we shall be con-

scious of forming the habit. But it will soon pass into normal spiritual health, and it must never be worshiped as a conscious process.

Our Method

> When you pray, do not use vain repetitions as the heathen do. For they think that they will be heard for their many words. (Matthew 6:7)

Beware of the trick of exposition which externalizes Scripture so that we teach but never learn its lessons. That means just this—we take a description from missionary literature of the heathen prayer roll with its yards of prayers that wind and unwind, and we dexterously show how futile and pathetic this is, and so on, and by our very method remove it from its homecoming benefit. Let the words come home to us personally in their New Testament setting, "When you pray, do not use vain repetitions." Our Lord prayed the same prayer, using the same words, three times in the Garden of Gethsemane, and He gave the disciples a form of prayer which He knew would be repeated throughout the Christian centuries—so it cannot be mere repetition or the form of words that He is referring to. The latter half of the verse comes home better for personal purposes—"they think that they will be heard for their many words"—that is, do not rely on your earnestness as the ground for being heard. This is a much-needed caution because it is so subtle a thing, this thing called earnestness. As the Reverend John McNeil, the great Scottish evangelist, said about the student of Elisha after he had lost the ax head (2 Kings 6:1–7), "If he had been of the modern school, Elisha would have said 'whack awa' wi' the stump, mon; earnestness is everything!' " Earnestness is not by any means everything; it is very often a subtle form of pious self-idolatry, because it is obsessed with the method and not with the Master. The phrase "pray through" often means working ourselves up into a frenzy of earnestness in which perspiration is taken for inspiration. It is a mistake to think we are heard on the basis of our earnestness. We are heard on the evangelical basis, "Therefore, brethren, having boldness to enter the Holiest by the blood of Jesus" (Hebrews 10:19).

Our Manner

In this manner, therefore, pray. (Matthew 6:9)

(At this particular point we are not dealing with what is known as the "Lord's Prayer"; that is dealt with subsequently.)

Our Lord wishes us to understand that all morbid excesses must be cut off, and the simple personal relationship allowed to react. When we pray, remember we pray to a person, "Our Father," not to a tendency, or for the resulting reflex action, and we pray for particular personal needs which are universal: "daily bread," "debts," "debtors," "deliverances" (verses 11–13), and we pray as citizens of a universal spiritual kingdom—"Yours is the kingdom" (verse 13), and the manner is bold, simple, but absolutely spiritual.

All through our Lord implies discipleship, or what we understand by an experience of regeneration. In other words, His death is the gateway for us into the life He lives and to which His teaching applies. Therefore to take our Lord's teaching and deny the need to be born from above is to produce a mockery, born of the very desire to do the opposite.

This section is presented as a stirring up and away from sentimental religiosity which is injurious to a degree that it becomes immoral, because it unfits for life instead of equipping for life, the life that is ever the result of our Lord's life in us.

The Pattern Prayer

Let this be how you pray: 'Our Father in heaven, Your name be revered, Your Reign begin, Your will be done on earth as in heaven! give us to-day our bread for the morrow, and forgive us our debts as we ourselves have forgiven our debtors, and lead us not into temptation but deliver us from evil.' (Matthew 6:9–13, MOFFAT)

(This translation may serve to rouse complacent attention to reexamine the very familiar form of words.)

This pattern prayer is our Lord's lesson on prayer in answer to a prayer: "One of His disciples said to Him, 'Lord, teach us to pray' " (Luke 11:1). It is well to remember that our Lord's disciples were used to prayer and religious exercises from their earliest childhood, but contact with Jesus produced in them the realization of the reality of free prayer over and beyond the liturgical form. How similar is our condition: after we have received spiritual quickening and illumination from our Lord, our eloquence falters, our coherent praying falters into an unsyllabled lack of utterance, and in utter confusion of mind and chaos of spirit we come as helpless babes to our Father with the first prayer, "Lord, teach us to pray," and He teaches us the alphabet of all possible prayer. This sense of utter impoverishment spiritually is a blessed pain because it is pain that takes us to God and His gracious rule and kingdom.

"Blessed are the poor in spirit, for theirs is the kingdom of heaven" (Matthew 5:3).

Presentation of Ideas

In this manner, therefore, pray. (Matthew 6:9)

How blessed it is to begin at the beginning—spiritual minors, stripped of our rich and verbal devotional language, and impoverished into receptive teachableness. Let our minds, made fertile by reason of genuine humility, receive the ideas our Lord presents in this familiar pattern prayer, receive in wonder and reverence the simple idea of God's personal relationship to us, "Our Father. . . . Your Father knows the things you have need of before you ask Him" (verse 8). Our Father gathers us near Him in the secret place alone with our fears and apprehensions and foolishness and aspirations, and He rewards us. When we talk about the fatherhood of God, let us remember that the Lord Jesus is the exclusive way to the Father. That is not an idea to be inferred, but to be received: "No one comes to the Father except through Me" (John 14:6). We can get to God as Creator apart from Jesus Christ (Romans 1:20), but never to God as our Father except through Him. Let us receive this inspired idea of our Lord's right into our inmost willing hearts. Believe it, and pray in the confidence of it.

Again, let us receive the idea of praying about our personal requirements. What topics our Lord suggests! What emancipation and joy come to us when we receive the revelation from our Lord Himself that we pray about things which naturally we take as animals, trusting to our wits and instinct and intuition. How many of us are like the psalmist of old who wrote a paragraph of autobiography in the words, "I was so foolish and ignorant; I was like a beast before You" (Psalm 73:22). He does not mean an immoral beast, but just as a beast of the field taking its fill without the slightest apprehension of God. When we ask grace before a meal, let us remember that it is not to be a mere pious custom, but a real reception of the idea of Jesus that God enables us to receive our daily bread from Him. I sometimes wonder if there would be as much chronic indigestion as there is if we received our ideas from God as Jesus would have us do.

Again, let us receive the idea of the personal rule of our Lord, "Your kingdom come" (Matthew 6:10). This does not mean bringing to Christian discipleship our natural ideas of the kingdom, but receiving our Lord's idea of the kingdom, or rule, or realm of God, a heavenly and eternal kingdom, which will only be established on earth as it is in heaven by our willing reception and reverence.

Presentation of Language

When you pray, say, "Our Father in heaven." (Luke 11:2)

Words are full of revelation when we do not simply recall or memorize them but receive them. Receive these words from Jesus: "Father," "heaven," "hallowed be Your name," "kingdom," "will"; there is all the vocabulary of the deity and dominion and disposition of Almighty God in relation to men in these words. Or take the words: "bread," "forgiveness," "debts," "temptation," "deliverance," "evil." In these words the primary psychological colors which portray the perplexing puzzles and problems of personal life, are all spelled out before our Father.

Or, lastly, look at such words as "power," "glory," "forever," "Amen,"*—in them there sounds the transcendent triumph truth that all is well, that God reigns and rules and rejoices, and His joy is our strength. What a rapturous

---

*Even if this clause is not in any of the oldest manuscripts, it is so universally used in the Christian church that it is not wise to miss it.

grammar class our Lord Jesus conducts when we go to His school of prayer and learn of Him!

Presentation of Faith

Your will be done on earth as it is in heaven. (Matthew 6:10)

It is not that our Lord gives us original thoughts, but that He gives spontaneous original life to all who receive from Him. Our Lord's very words, repeated by a simple receiver of His tuition, create the faith required for Christian perseverance. Receiving from Jesus and requesting Almighty God in obedience to Him, enables God, so to speak, to create the actual things prayed for. Faith worked out in this way is submissive, but how we miss the meaning of the New Testament words if we take them etymologically only, instead of in their evangelical accidence. Submission, for instance, means etymologically, surrender to another, but in the evangelical sense it means that I conduct myself actually among men as the submissive child of my Father in heaven.

There is an illustration of this subject in the pattern prayer: "If you forgive men their trespasses, your heavenly Father will also forgive you. But if you do not forgive men their trespasses, neither will your Father forgive your trespasses" (Matthew 6:14–15).

The forgiveness of a child of God is not placed on the grounds of the atonement of our Lord, but on the grounds that the child of God shows the same forgiveness to his fellows that God his Father has shown to him.

This is submission and perseverance and faith all worked into an intensely humble, sensible, actual, human life. We are delivered from sin that we might actually live as saints among people who treat us as we once treated our heavenly Father. Let us, with chastened and delighted hearts and lips, thank God that He has taught us in the pattern prayer of our Father, our fellowship, and our faith.

> Oh, long and dark the stairs I trod,
> With stumbling feet to find my God:
>
> Gaining a foothold bit by bit,
> Then slipping back and losing it:
>
> Never progressing, striving still,
> With weakening grasp and fainting will,
>
> Bleeding to climb to God: while He
> Serenely smiled, unnoting me.
>
> Then came a certain time when I
> Loosened my hold and fell thereby.
>
> Down to the lowest step my fall,
> As if I had not climbed at all.
>
> And while I lay despairing there,
> I heard a footfall on the stair,
>
> In the same path where I, dismayed,
> Faltered and fell and lay afraid.
>
> And lo! when hope had ceased to be,
> My God came down the stairs to me.

Private Prayer

When you pray, go into your room and shut the door, pray to your Father who is in secret, and your Father who sees what is in secret will reward you. (Matthew 6:6, MOFFAT)

This verse presents our Lord's recommendation and His revelation.

Our Lord's recommendation naturally presents itself in these ways: A disciple should have a special habit, a selected place, a secret silence, and a disciple should strenuously pray.

So we will construe all we have to consider according to this outline.

A Disciple Should Have a Special Habit

When you pray.

Beware of the impression that could be expressed something like this: "But it is so difficult to get time." Of course it is, we have to make time, and that means effort, and effort makes us conscious of the need to reorganize our general ways. It will facilitate matters to remember, even if it humbles us, that we take time to eat our breakfast and our dinner. Most of the difficulty in forming a special habit is that we will not discipline ourselves. Read carefully this quotation from Professor William James' brilliant *Text-Book of Psychology,* and apply it to the matter of prayer:

The great thing, then, in all education, is to make our nervous system our ally instead of our enemy. It is to fund and capitalize our acquisitions, and live at ease upon the interest of the fund. For this we must make automatic and habitual, as early as possible, as many useful actions as we can, and guard against the growing into ways that are likely to be disadvantageous to us, as we should guard against the plague. . . . The first (maxim) is that in the acquisition of a new habit, or the leaving off of an old one, we must take care to launch ourselves with as strong and decided an initiative as possible. . . . The second maxim is:

Never suffer an exception to occur till the new habit is securely rooted in your life. . . . A third maxim may be added to the preceding pair: Seize the very first possible opportunity to act on every resolution you make, and on every emotional prompting you may experience in the direction of the habit you aspire to gain.

Let us apply that lesson right away to ourselves, and take our Lord's advice home until it becomes character. You say you cannot get up early in the morning; well, a very good thing to do is to get up in order to prove that you cannot! This does not contradict at all what has already been said, namely, that we must not put earnestness in the place of God. It means that we have to understand that our bodily mechanism is made by God, and that when we are regenerated He does not give us another body. We have the same body, and therefore the way we use our wits in order to learn a secular thing is the way to learn any spiritual thing. "When you pray—" *begin now.*

A Disciple Should Have a Selected Place

Go into your room.

Did you ever say anything like this to yourself, "It is so difficult to select a place"? What about the time when you were in love, was it impossible to select a place to meet in? No, it was far from impossible; and beware of self-indulgence. Think how long our Lord has waited for you. You have seen Him in your visions, now pray to Him; get a place, not a mood, but a definite material place and resort to it constantly, and pray to God as His Spirit in you will help you. Bring to earth the promised life you have longed for, curb your impulsive, undisciplined, wayward nature to His use, and rule your body like a king where now, even in strength and honesty, you walk sentenced to be a prey to baser and less spiritual things. Do not say, "If I only had so and so," you have not got so and so; but you can, if you will, select a place where you are. We can always do what we want to do if we want to do it sufficiently keenly. Do it *now.* "Enter into your room"; and remember, it is a place selected to pray in, not to make little addresses in, or for any purpose other than to pray in—never forget that.

A Disciple Should Have a Secret Silence
  When you have shut your door.

"It is so difficult to get quiet," you say. What about the time when you were ill? Oh, it can be done, but you must know how to shut the door. Remember the devil may not know what you know until you tell him, so do not say to your friends, or your household, or your landlady, as the case may be, "I am just going to pray." That's too much like the playacting we have already been warned about. No, it is to be a selected place, a secret shut-in place, where no one ever guesses what you are doing. Quietists and mystics are inclined to grave danger, but they say and write some very fine things. For instance, Molinos says this, and it is exactly suitable for being quiet in the shut-in place:

> The way of inward peace is in all things to be conformed to the pleasure and disposition of the divine will. Such as would have all things succeed and come to pass according to their own fancy, are not come to know this way, and therefore lead a harsh and bitter life, always restless or out of humor, without treading in the way of peace which consists in a total conformity to the will of God.

There is another vital moral matter mentioned in Matthew 5:23–24:

"If you bring your gift to the altar, and there remember that your brother has something against you, leave your gift there before the altar, and go your way. First be reconciled to your brother, and then come and offer your gift."

If you have incurred a debt and not paid it, or cared about paying it, or have spoken in the wrong mood to another, or been vindictive—these and similar things pro-duce a wrong temper of soul, it is no use trying to pray until you do what the Lord says. The one thing that keeps us from doing it is pride, and pride has never yet prayed in the history of humanity.

> I walk down the Valley of Silence,
>   Down the dim voiceless valley alone,
> And I hear not a sound of a footstep
>   Around me but God's and my own,
> And the hush of my heart is as holy
>   As bowers whence angels have flown.
>
> In the hush of the Valley of Silence,
>   I hear all the songs that I sing,
> And the notes float down the dim Valley
>   Till each finds a word for a wing,
> That to men like the dove of the deluge,
>   The message of peace they may bring.

A Disciple Should Strenuously Pray

Pray to your Father who is in the secret place.

The objection is easily brought forward: "It is so difficult to concentrate one's thought," yet what about the time you were working for that position, or to pass that examination? All our excuses arise from some revealing form of self-indul-gence. To pray strenuously needs careful cultivation. We have to learn the most natural methods of expressing ourselves to our Father. In the beginning we may clamor for presents and for things, and our Father encourages us in these elementary petitions until we learn to understand Him better, then we begin to talk to Him in free reverent intimacy, understanding more and more His wonderful nature. "Your Father knows the things you have need of before you ask Him" (Matthew 6:8).

The real reason for prayer is intimacy of relation with our Father. There are many ways that help. Let me give some out of my own experience, although it is unsatisfactory to do this because others are apt to imitate instead of assimilate. To rewrite the Psalms into a free language of expression of one's own has proved to me a valuable treasure house of self-expression to God. At times, though very rarely, I like a horology such as Bishop Andrews' devotions; but I find a most beneficial exercise in secret prayer before the Father, is to write things down so that I see exactly what I think and want to say. Only those who have tried these ways know the ineffable benefit of such strenuous times in secret.

Lord, what a change within us one short hour
Spent in Thy presence will prevail to make,
What heavy burdens from our bosoms take,
What parched grounds refresh as with a shower!
We kneel, and all around us seems to lower;
We rise, and all, the distant and the near,
Stands forth in sunny outline, brave and clear;
We kneel, how weak, we rise how full of power.
Why therefore should we do ourselves this wrong
Or others that we are not always strong,
That we are ever overborne with care,
That we should ever weak or heartless be,
Anxious or troubled, when with us in Prayer,
And joy and strength and courage are with Thee?

Such, then, are our Lord's recommendations for private prayer. Now let us look at His revelation regarding private prayer.

The Father's Discerning Disposition

Your Father who sees in secret.

The revelation here is of the free kingdom of love. There is no blind creaturely subjection to a creator but the free kingdom in which the one who prays is conscious of limit only through the moral nature of the Father's holiness. It is a revelation of pure joyousness in which the child of God pours into the Father's bosom the cares which give pain and anxiety that He may solve the difficulties. Too often we imagine that God lives in a place where He only repairs our broken treasures, but Jesus reveals that it is quite otherwise; He discerns all our difficulties and solves them before us. We are not beggars on the one hand or spiritual customers on the other; we are God's children, and we just stay before Him with our broken treasures or our pain and watch Him mend or heal in such a way that we understand Him better.

The Father's Delighted Doings

Your Father . . . will Himself reward you openly.

Think of the unfathomable bliss of the revelation that we shall perceive our Father solving our problems, and shall understand Him; it is the reward of the joyous time of prayer. In all the temptations that contend in our hearts, and amidst the things that meet us in the providence of God which seem to involve a contradiction of His fatherhood, the secret place convinces us that He is our Father and that He is righteousness and love, and we remain not only unshaken but we receive our reward with an intimacy that is unspeakable and full of glory.

Give me the lowest place, not that I dare
Ask for the lowest place, but Thou hast died
That I might live and share
    Thy glory by Thy side.
Give me the lowest place, or if for me
That lowest place too high, make one more low
Where I may sit and see
    My God and love Thee so.

Public Prayer

I tell you another thing: if two of you agree on
earth about anything you pray for, it will be done for
you by my Father in heaven, for where two or three
have gathered in My name, I am there among them.
(Matthew 18:19–20, MOFFAT)

These words are so simple, and so remarkable for guidance and instruction regarding public prayer meetings that
our departure from their counsel is a great mystery. It is com-
paratively easy to think or say apt things about private
prayer, but it is not so easy to say things about public prayer.
The reason probably is that few of us are willing to carry the
cross of public prayer, or at least if we do, we repeat aloud,
to a large extent, our own private concerns, which are much
better told in secret and alone. It is easier, too, to evade self-
consciousness in private prayer. Emancipation from self-consciousness is like a deliverance from a terrible sickness, and
one gets rather alarmed at the slightest symptom of it again.
Probably this is the reason why many Christians, who ought
to be the strength and safeguard of a public prayer meeting
in a community of Christians, are not so. They keep silent
and just one or two who have merely the gift of devotional

language are allowed to dominate the prayer meeting. And the midweek prayer meeting is given up and becomes the mid-week service. We must remember that there is a sacrifice of prayer as well as a sacrifice of praise.

In the words of Matthew 18:19–20, our Lord conveys simple and plain guidance in regard to the arrangement and the atmosphere of a public prayer meeting.

The Arrangement of the Public Prayer Meeting

It is never easy to pray in public and so few of us are willing to have our nervous equilibrium upset for the sake of fulfilling a request of our Lord's. But why should not our nervous equilibrium be upset? Why should many public prayer meetings be ruined by the long-winded brother who does not really pray but discourses on theology and insists on doctrine? We all mourn this abuse of the public prayer meeting. It is a contemptible thing because it usurps the time of the saints. Yet the real rebuke ought to lie at the door of the humble saints who should pray when the opportunity is given, and thus allow no occasion to the Enemy.

Agreement in Purpose on Earth

Again I say to you that if two of you agree on earth.

We need to know this simple, direct truth about praying in public. It is perilously easy to make public prayer the mere fringe of devotion to what we are pleased to think of as the real center of the meeting. Agreement in purpose on earth must not be taken to mean a predetermination to agree together to storm God's fort doggedly till He yields. It is far from right to agree beforehand over what we want, and then go to God and wait, not until He gives us His mind about the matter, but until we extort from Him permission to do what we had made up our minds to do before we prayed. We should rather agree to ask God to convey His mind and meaning to us in regard to the matter. Agreement in purpose on earth is not a public presentation of persistent begging which knows no limit, but a prayer which is conscious that it is limited through the moral nature of the Holy Spirit. It is really "symphonizing" on earth with our Father who is in heaven.

Asking in Prayer on Earth

Concerning anything that they ask.

It is a very important matter of instruction to be guided in our asking in public. To facilitate this end it is better to have numbers of short prayers than a few long ones, and numbers of short prayers not on the same subject, but on many subjects, so that the whole meeting may agree with the petitioners. There are many simple helps in this matter, such as the leader of the meeting suggesting topics, or asking the people themselves to quote a verse of Scripture, or anything that will enable the people to pronounce aloud the requests that are in their hearts. It is never necessary in a public prayer meeting for one to present all the petitions as it is in a public service; there one person has to make the presentation in prayer of the needs of the congregation, and of the much larger sphere of humanity; but that is public worship. As in private matters, our Lord's instruction on public prayer is essentially simple.

Public Prayer Is Answered in Particular from Heaven

It will be done for them by My Father in heaven.

This reminds us very forcibly of our Lord's statement that "everyone who asks receives" (Luke 11:10). Prayer to the natural man who has not been born from above is so simple, so stupid, and so supernatural as to be at once taboo.

Strange to say, the reasons he gives for objecting to prayer are the very reasons that give it its true nature. Prayer is simple, as simple as a child making known its wants to its parents (see Matthew 11:25). Prayer is stupid, because it is not according to common sense—it is certain that God does things in answer to prayer, and this, common sense naturally says, is ridiculous (see James 5:16); prayer is supernatural because it relies entirely on God (see 1 John 5:14–15).

Let us then go into the hearty cultivation of public prayer, making our requests known before one another as well as before God, and thus securing the answers in partic-ular from heaven.

The Atmosphere of the Public Prayer Meeting

Atmosphere is not only something assimilated, but something we help to produce, and is both subjective and objective. To ask the Spirit of God to take up His abode in the atmosphere of a meeting is not at all unnecessary; the idea of "sacred places" can be easily abused but it does not follow that there is no such thing as a sacred place. For instance, it is easier to pray in a place used only for prayer than it is to pray in a theater.

"Where two or three are gathered together . . ." (Matthew 18:20). Christian secrecy when made a conscious effort is a snare and a delusion because it leads to segrega-tion, not to congregation. The "together" aspect of the Christian life is continually insisted on in the New Testament. God "raised us up together, and made us sit together in the heavenly places in Christ Jesus" (Ephesians 2:6). We attain together, "to the measure of the stature of the fullness of Christ" (Ephesians 4:13), and the writer to the Hebrews warns us not to forsake "the assembling of ourselves together" (Hebrews 10:25). There is nothing of the special coterie about the Christian prayer meeting. It is not a "hole-and-corner" secret society, but a public meeting for one purpose, assembling together to pray, and the assembly must be akin to each other.

"In My name," this oft-repeated phrase means, "in My nature." It is a sad fact that through pique or self-opinionatedness a man sometimes finds himself and his self-love wounded in the prayer meeting with his brethren, so he separates himself and has a little prayer meeting in his own home. That is certainly not assembling together "in my name," but is assembling together from a motive of defiance. "In My name" refers to those who are born of the Spirit of God; the nature of God is imparted to the recipient so that when we pray in His name we pray in His nature (see Romans 5:5).

"I am there in the midst of them." A wonderful picture—a group of our Lord's children around the knees of the heavenly Father, making their requests known in familiarity, in awe and reverence, in simplicity and confidence in Him, and in humble certainty that He is there.

Our prayers should be in accordance with the nature of God, therefore the answers are not in accordance with our nature but with His. We are apt to forget this and to say, without thinking, that God does not answer prayer; but He always answers prayer, and when we are in close communion with Him we know that we have not been misled.

> Stir me, oh! stir me, Lord, I care not how,
>   But stir my heart in passion for the world!
> Stir me to give, to go—but most to pray;
>   Stir, till the blood-red banner is unfurled
> O'er lands that still in heathen darkness lie,
> O'er deserts where no cross is lifted high.

Stir me, oh! stir me, Lord, till prayer is pain—
 Till prayer is joy—till prayer turns into praise!
Stir me, till heart and will and mind—yea, all
 Is wholly Thine to use through all the day.
Stir, till I learn to pray 'exceedingly':
Stir, till I learn to wait expectantly.

Patient and Prevailing Prayer

So far we have been dealing with the aspects of prayer which are more or less easy of statement. We enter now into an aspect which is more difficult to state. Prayer is the outcome of our apprehension of the nature of God, and the means whereby we assimilate more and more of His mind.

We must here remind ourselves of the fundamental matters of our Christian relationship, namely, that in a Christian, faith and common sense are molded in one person by devotion to the mastership of Jesus Christ. This necessitates not conscious adherence to principles, but concentrated obedience to the Master. Faith does not become its own object—that produces fanaticism; but it becomes the means whereby God unveils His purposes to us (see Romans 12:2).

Our Lord in instructing the disciples in regard to prayer presented them with three pictures (see Luke 11:1–13 and 18:1–8), and strangely puzzling pictures they are until we understand their meaning. They are the pictures of an unkind friend, an unnatural father, and an unjust judge. Like many of our Lord's answers, these pictures seem no answer at all at first; they seem evasions; but we find that in answering our inarticulate questions our Lord presents His answer to the reality discernible to conscience, and not to logic.

He said to them, "Which of you shall have a friend, and go to him at midnight and say to him, 'Friend, lend me three loaves; for a friend of mine has come to me on his journey, and I have nothing to set before him'; And he will answer from within and say, 'Do not trouble me; the door is now shut, and my children are with me in bed; I cannot rise and give to you.' I say to you, though he will not rise and give to him because he is his friend, yet because of his persistence he will rise and give him as many as he needs" (Luke 11:5–8).

This is plainly a picture of what the Heavenly Father does sometimes seem to be like, and the problem our Lord faced in the minds of His disciples has to be faced by us at all times. He says, in effect, "I know that to your mind the heavenly Father will appear at times as an unkind friend, but let Me assure you He is not; and even if He were, if you went on praying long enough, He would answer you. There is a reason which He cannot explain to you just now, because the explanation only comes through the experience of discipline which you will understand someday."

It appears as if God were sometimes most unnatural. We ask Him to bless our lives and bring benedictions, and what immediately follows turns everything into actual ruin. The reason is that before God can make the heart into a garden of the Lord, He has to plow it, and that will take away a great deal of natural beauty. If we interpret God's designs by our desires, we will say He gave us a scorpion when we asked an egg, and a serpent when we asked a fish, and a stone when we asked for bread. But our Lord indicates that such thinking and speaking is too hasty. It is not born of faith or reliance on God. "Everyone who asks receives."

Our Lord says that God the Father will give the Holy Spirit much more readily than we would give good gifts to our children, and the Holy Spirit not only brings us into the zone of God's influence but into intimate relationship with Him personally, so that by the slow discipline of prayer the choices of our free wills become the preordinations of His almighty order. When we say we have no faith, we simply betray our own case, namely, that we have no confidence in God at all, for faith is born of confidence in Him.

The Unjust Judge

He spoke a parable to them, that men always ought to pray and not lose heart, saying, "There was in a certain city a judge who did not fear God, nor regard man. Now there was a widow in that city; and she came to him, saying, 'Get justice for me from my adversary.' And he would not for a while; but afterward he said within himself, 'Though I do not fear God nor regard man, yet because this widow troubles me I will avenge her, lest by her continual coming she weary me.' " Then the Lord said, "Hear what the unjust judge said. And shall God not avenge His own elect who cry out day and night to Him, though He bears long with them? I tell you that He will avenge them speedily. Nevertheless, when the Son of Man comes, will He really find faith on the earth?" (Luke 18:1–8)

In this illustration our Lord recognizes by implication that God does seem at times utterly powerless and unjust, but He says, in effect, "God is not unjust, He is longsuffering." Our Lord does not attempt to answer our questions on our level, He lifts us up to His level and allows us to make no excuse for not continuing in prayer. The battle in prayer is against two things in the earthlies: wandering thoughts, and lack of intimacy with God's character as revealed in His Word. Neither can be cured at once, but they can be cured by discipline. In mental work it takes time to gain the victory over wandering thoughts which do not come necessarily through supernatural agents, but through lack of concentration. Concentration is only learned little by little, and the more impulsive you are, the less concentrated you will be. So when wandering thoughts come in prayer, don't ask God to forgive you, but stop having them. It is not a bit of use to ask God to keep out wandering thoughts, you must keep them out. And in regard to God's Word, see you take time to know it; God's Spirit will give you an understanding of His nature, make His Word spirit and life to you.

Our counsel for patient prayer is to note the importunity which our Lord insists on in each of these illustrations, and to remember it is importunity on behalf of another, not on our own account. Our importunity must be intercessory, and the whole power of our intercession lies in the certainty that prayer will be answered. Intercessory prayer based on the redemption enables God to create that which He can create in no other way; it is a strenuous business demanding the undivided energy of mind and heart. The effect of our prayers on ourselves is the building up of our character in the understanding of the character of God. That is why we need patience in prayer. We cannot "by one wild bound, clear the numberless ascensions of starry stairs." Prayer is not logical—it is a mysterious moral working of the Holy Spirit.

The Unnatural Father

I say to you, ask, and it will be given to you; seek, and you will find; knock, and it will be opened to you. For everyone who asks receives, and he who seeks finds, and to him who knocks it will be opened. If a son asks for bread from any father among you, will he give him a stone? Or if he asks for a fish, will he give him a serpent instead of a fish? Or if he asks for an egg, will he offer him a scorpion? If you then, being evil, know how to give good gifts to your children, how much more will your heavenly Father give the Holy Spirit to those who ask Him? (Luke 11:9–13)

Just here at the conclusion of these pictures the case of Job is of peculiar significance. In Job's case there was every element to make him conceive of God as an unkind friend, an unnatural Father, and an unjust judge; but through everything Job stuck to his belief in the character of God. Job lost his hereditary creed, which was that God blessed and prospered physically and materially the man who trusted in Him, but his words, "Though He slay me, yet will I trust Him" (Job 13:15), prove how tenaciously he clung to God.

At the conclusion of the book of Job these striking words occur, "The Lord restored Job's losses when he prayed for his friends. Indeed the Lord gave Job twice as much as he had before" (Job 42:10). So the question to ask yourself, which, though it may be ungrammatical, is very pointed: Have you come to *when* yet? Have you entered into the high-priestly union of praying for your friends? *When* you do, God will turn your captivity.

> Go thou into thy closet; shut thy door,
>   And pray to Him in secret; He will hear.
> But think not thou, by one wild bound, to clear
> The numberless ascensions, more and more,
> Of starry stairs that must be climbed, before

Thou comest to the Father's likeness near;
And bendest down to kiss the feet so dear
That, step by step, their mounting flights passed o'er.
Be thou content, if on thy weary need
There falls a sense of showers and of the Spring;
A hope that makes it possible to fling
Sickness aside, and go and do the deed:
For highest aspiration will not lead
Unto the calm beyond all questioning.

Under the heading of prevailing prayer we come really to the subject of subconscious prayer. We mean by subconscious prayer the prayer that goes on in our unconscious mind, only occasionally bursting up into the conscious. Romans 8:26–28 is the classical example of this:

"The Spirit also helps in our weaknesses. For we do not know what we should pray for as we ought, but the Spirit Himself makes intercession for us with groanings which cannot be uttered. Now He who searches the hearts knows what the mind of the Spirit is, because He makes intercession for the saints according to the will of God. And we know that all things work together for good to those who love God, to those who are the called according to His purpose."

"Praying always with all prayer and supplication in the Spirit . . ." (Ephesians 6:18). Prayer "in the Spirit" is not meditation, it is not reverie; it is being filled with the Holy Spirit who brings us as we pray into perfect union before God, and this union manifests itself in "perseverance and supplication for all saints." Every saint of God knows those times when in closest communion with God nothing is articulated, and yet there seems to be an absolute intimacy not so much between God's mind and his mind as between God's Spirit and his spirit.

The conscious and the subconscious life of our Lord is explained perhaps in this way. Our Lord's subconscious life was deity; and only occasionally when He was on earth did the subconscious burst up into His conscious life. The subconscious life of the saint is the Holy Spirit, and in such moments of prayer as are alluded to in Romans 8:26-28, there is an uprush of communion with God into the consciousness of the saint. The only explanation of this is that the Holy Spirit in the saint is communicating prayers which cannot be uttered, and acquaints us with the—

Unrealized Particulars of Prayer

The Spirit also helps our weaknesses. For we do not know what we should pray for as we ought, but the Spirit Himself makes intercession for us with groanings which cannot be uttered. (Romans 8:26)

This verse details for us our infirmities, our inability, and our Intercessor. The Holy Spirit has special prayers in every individual saint which bring him or her at times under the powerful searching of God to find out what is the mind of the Spirit. This searching of the heart is bewildering at first because we are tortured by our unsyllabled lack of utterance, but we are soon comforted by the realization that God is searching our hearts not for the convicting of sin, but to find out what is the mind of the Spirit.

"He who searches the hearts knows what the mind of the Spirit is, because He makes intercession for the saints according to the will of God" (8:27).

Unrivaled Power of Prayer

This verse describes the Spirit's intercession before God and identification with God going on in the personality of the saint, apart altogether from the saint's conscious power of understanding. This can safely be called "speechless prayer"; we wait before God, lying fallow, as it were, while He answers the prayer the Holy Spirit is praying in us. The prayer of our Lord in John 17 is closely allied with the inter-cession of the Holy Spirit, and this High Priestly Prayer explains many, if not all, of the mysterious things a saint has to go through.

"We know that all things work together for good to those who love God, to those who are the called according to His purpose" (8:28).

This verse presents the—

Unrecognized Providence of Prayer

The shrine of conscious life is placed in a sacredness of circumstances engineered by God whereby He secures our effectual calling. That God engineers our circumstances for us if we accept His purpose in Christ Jesus is a thought of great practical moment.

Allow yourself to think for a little that you are to be a walking, living edition of the prayers of the Holy Spirit. No wonder God urges us to walk in the light! No wonder His Spirit prays in us and makes intercessions with groanings we cannot utter. We may feel burdened or we may not; we may consciously know nothing about it. The point is that God puts us into circumstances where He can answer the prayers of His Son and of the Holy Spirit. Remember the prayer of Jesus is "that they may be one as We are." That is a oneness of personality in which individuality is completely transfigured; it is independence lost and identity revealed.

It is well to remember that it is the "together" of circum-stances that works for good. God changes our circum-stances; sometimes they are bright, sometimes they are the opposite. God makes them work together for our good, so that in each particular set of circumstances we are in, the Spirit of God has a better chance to pray the particular prayers that suit His designs. The reason is only known to God, not to us.

In James 5:16–18 there is instruction for everyone. This might be called successful prayer. We are told that the great man Elijah is as a little man, "Elijah was a man with a nature like ours" (verse 17), and that the great man prayed just as a little man, "and he prayed earnestly," and the great man was answered just as a little man will be answered, by God. The phrase "he prayed earnestly" is literally, "he prayed in prayer."

Intercessory prayer is part of the sovereign purpose of God. If there were no saints praying for us, our lives would be infinitely balder than they are. Consequently, the responsibility of those who never intercede and who are withholding blessing from other lives is truly appalling. The subject of intercessory prayer is weakened by the neglect of the idea with which we ought to start. We take for granted that prayer is preparation for work, whereas prayer is *the* work. We scarcely believe what the Bible reveals, namely, that through intercessory prayer God creates on the grounds of the redemption; it is His chosen way of working. We lean to our own understanding, or we bank on service and do away with prayer, and consequently by succeeding in the external we fail in the eternal, because in the eternal we succeed only by prevailing prayer.

Perils of Prayer

In conclusion it is as well to note one or two points in regard to "The Perils of Prayer." Luke 22:31 reveals not only the possibility of Satan's praying, but of his prayers being answered, "Satan has asked for you, that he may sift you as wheat;" and in Psalm 106:14–15, we have the prayer of sensuality. In both these instances prayer was answered. Satan was allowed to sift Peter and the other disciples, with the result that after the resurrection they were ready to receive the Holy Spirit (see John 20:22), and we read that God gave the children of Israel their request, but "sent leanness into their soul."

First John 5:16 deals with prayer and will. "If anyone sees his brother sinning a sin which does not lead to death, he will ask, and He will give him life for those who commit sin not leading to death. There is sin leading to death. I do not say that he should pray about that." Intercessory prayer for one who is sinning prevails, God says so. The will of the man prayed for does not come into question at all. He is connected with God by prayer, and prayer on the basis of the redemption sets the connection working and God gives life. There is, however, a distinct limitation put to intercession—"I do not say that he should pray about that." This is also illustrated in the prayers of Abraham for Sodom (See Genesis 18:16–33). The only way in which we can discern this limit of intercession is by living in continual communion with God and not in any wise leaning to our own understanding.

There are, so to speak, two types of redemptive effects in answer to intercession: the first where souls are "saved, yet so as through fire"; and the second where they are saved and brought into requisition for God in this life. The intercession for all men is on the former line and the intercession for particular cases is on the second. Beware of the philosophy with regard to the human will bringing factors in here that are distinctly absent in God's revelation about prayer. The fundamental basis of the human will deep down is inclined toward God, and prayer works wonders fundamentally. The prayer of the feeblest saint on earth who lives in the Spirit and keeps right with God is a terror to Satan. The very powers of darkness are paralyzed by prayer; no spiritualistic seance can succeed in the presence of a humble praying saint. No wonder Satan tries to keep our minds fussy in active work till we cannot think in prayer. It is a vital necessity for Christians to think along the lines on which they pray. The philosophy of prayer is that prayer is *the* work.

Jesus Christ carries on intercession for us in heaven; the Holy Spirit carries on intercession in us on earth; and we the saints have to carry on intercession for all men.

There remains one further matter it is well to note, namely—

Idle Prayer

This subject of idle prayer is referred to by Charles Kingsley in a letter written April 25, 1852:

> You have said boldly, in words which pleased me much, though I differ from them—that I ought not to ask you to try to cure self-seeking by idle prayer—as if a man by taking thought could add one cubit to his stature. I was pleased with the words; because they show me that you have found that there is a sort of prayer which is idle prayer, and that you had sooner not pray at all than in that way. Now of idle prayer I think there are two kinds: one of fetish prayer, when by praying we seek to alter the will of God concerning us. This is, and has been, and will be common enough and idle enough. For if the will of Him concerning us be good, why should we alter it? If bad,

what use praying to such a being at all? . . . Another, of praying to oneself to change oneself; by which I mean the common method of trying by prayer to excite oneself into a state, a frame, an experience. This, too, is common enough among Protestants and papists, as well as among Unitarians and rationalists. Indeed, some folks tell us that the great use of prayer is its reflex action on ourselves, and inform us that we can thus, by taking thought, add certain cubits to our stature. God knows the temptation to believe it is great. I feel it deeply. Nevertheless I am not of that belief.

From *Charles Kingsley: His Letters and Memories of His Life.* The whole letter is well worth reading.

It is a great privilege to be disciplined by loneliness. Thank you, Lord!

5

The Discipline of Loneliness

Now I am no longer in the world, but these are in the world, and I come to You. Holy Father, keep through Your name those whom You have given Me, that they may be one, as We are. . . . I have given them Your word; and the world has hated them because they are not of the world, just as I am not of the world. I do not pray that You should take them out of the world, but that You should keep them from the evil one. They are not of the world, just as I am not of the world. Sanctify them by Your truth. Your word is truth. As You sent Me into the world, I also have sent them into the world. (John 17:11, 14–18)

The friendship of a soul who walks alone with God is as abiding as God Himself, and, in degree, as terrible. What a volume of meaning is in these words, so simple in state-ment—"And looking at Jesus as He walked, he said, 'Behold the Lamb of God!' " (John 1:36). Charles Kingsley speaks of his wife as his "dear dread." A friend whose contact and whose memory does not make us ever do our best is one in name only. Friendship to a soul undisciplined by loneliness

151

is a precarious sea on which many have been lost, and on whose shores the wrecks of many human hearts lie rotting.

Solitude with God repairs the damage done by the fret and noise and clamor of the world. To have been on the mount with God means that we carry with us an exhilaration, an incommunicable awe. We do not descend to the valley, no matter how low the walk of the feet may have to be, no matter how perplexing the demon-tossed may be around us, no matter if the cross awaits us in the shadows.

"Now it was so, when Moses came down from Mount Sinai (and the two tablets of the Testimony were in Moses' hand when he came down from the mountain), that Moses did not know that the skin of his face shone while he talked with Him" (Exodus 34:29). "They marveled. And they realized that they had been with Jesus" (Acts 4:13).

The disaster of shallowness ultimately follows the spiritual life that takes not the shining way upon the mount of God. Power from on high has the Highest as its source, and the solitudes of the Highest must never be departed from, or else that power will cease.

> Heart, heart, awake! The love that loveth all
> Maketh a deeper calm than Horeb's cave:—
> God in thee,—*can* His children's folly gall?
> Love may be hurt, but shall not love be brave?
> Thy holy silence sinks in dews of balm;
> Thou art my solitude, my mountain-calm!
>
> *George Mac Donald*

Loneliness marks the child of God. In tumult, in trouble, in disaster, in pestilence, in destruction, in fighting with wild beasts, the child of God abides under the shadow of the Almighty,

Singing hymns unbidden,
   Till the world is wrought
To sympathy with hopes and fears it heeded not.

Shelley

The child of God who walks alone with Him is not depen-
dent on places and moods, but carries to the world the perpetual mystery of a dignity, unruffled, and unstung by insult,
untouched by shame and martyrdom. Robert Browning
describes him in "An Epistle Containing the Strange Medical
Experience of Karshish, the Arab Physician":

I probed the sore as thy disciple should:
"How, beast," said I, "this stolid carelessness
Sufficeth thee, when Rome is on her march
To stamp out like a little spark thy town,
Thy tribe, thy crazy tale and thee at once?"
He merely looked with his large eyes on me.
The man is apathetic, you deduce?
Contrariwise, he lives both old and young,
Able and weak, affects the very brutes
And birds—how say I? flowers of the field—
As a wise workman recognizes tools
In a master's workshop, loving what they make.

The very God! think, Abib; dost thou think?
So, the All-Great, were the All-Loving too—
So, through the thunder comes a human voice
Saying, "O heart I made, a heart beats here!
Face, my hands fashioned, see it in myself!
Thou hast no power nor mayest conceive of mine,
But love I gave thee, with myself to love,
And thou must love me who have died for thee!"
The madman saith He said so: it is strange.

Browning

The culture of the entirely sanctified life is often misunderstood. The discipline of that life consists of suffering, loneliness, patience and prayer. How many who started with the high ecstasy of vision have ended in the disasters of shallowness! Time, the world, and God fire out the fools. Our Lord was thirty years preparing for three years' service. The modern stamp is three hours of preparation for thirty years of service. John the Baptist and Paul were trained in the massive solitudes of the desert, as are all characters of God's heroic mold.

> . . . not in vain His seers
> Have dwelt in solitudes and known that God
> High up in open silence and thin air
> More presently reveals him, having set
> His chiefest temples on the mountain-tops,
> His kindling altar in the hearts of men,
> And these I knew with peace and lost with pain,
> Lamented, and in dreams was my desire
> For the flood Jordan, for the running sound
> And broken glitters of the midnight moon.
>
> F. W. H. Myers

Thus does Frederick Myers make John the Baptist soliloquize in prison. And again he touches Paul in soliloquy—

> Oh the regret, the struggle and the failing!
> Oh the days desolate and useless years!
> Vows in the night, so fierce and unavailing!
> Stings of my shame and passion of my tears!

> How have I seen in Araby Orion,
> Seen without seeing, till he set again,

Known the night-noise and the thunder of the lion;
   Silence and sounds of the prodigious plain!

How have I knelt with arms of my aspiring
   Lifted all night in irresponsive air,
Dazed and amazed with overmuch desiring,
   Blank with the utter agony of prayer!

In the momentous crisis of entire sanctification and the baptism of the Holy Spirit and fire, all heaven is opened and the soul is drunk with ecstasy—yet that is but the introduction to a new relationship. Entirely sanctified soul, alone with God, suffering with Jesus, do you hear Him say, "You do not know what you ask. Are you able to drink the cup that I am about to drink, and be baptized with the baptism that I am baptized with?" (Matthew 20:22). The world is cursed with holiness preachers who have never trembled under awesome Sinai, or lain prostrate in shame before Calvary and had the vile ownership of themselves strangled to death in the rare air heights of Pentecost. Testify to what the Lord has done for you, but at the peril of being cast away as reprobate silver, presume to preach or teach what you have not bought by suffering. Out on the disastrous shallowness that teaches and preaches *experiences!* The true holiness preacher is one whose experience has led him to know that he is charged with the oracles of God, and, backed by Jehovah, an awful woe is on him if he preaches not the gospel.

There is a solitude of despair, a solitude of sin—a vast curse black with the wrath of God, moaning with the pride of hatred; there is a solitude which is the aftermath of spent vice and exhausted self-love. There is no God in such solitudes, only an exhausting pessimism and a great despair.

These solitudes produce the wayward, wandering cries so prevalent among human beings. At one time, striking his fist at the throne of God, that lonely soul cries:

> I would ne'er have striven
> As thus with thee in prayer in my sore need.
> Oh! lift me as a wave, a leaf, a cloud!
> I fall upon the thorns of life! I bleed!
>
> A heavy weight of hours has chained and bowed
> One too like thee: tameless, and swift, and proud.

Or again, in the utter exhaustion of companionless isolation:

> I could lie down like a tired child,
>   And weep away the life of care
> Which I have borne and yet must bear,
>   Till death like sleep might steal on me,
> And I might feel in the warm air
>   My cheek grow cold, and hear the sea
> Breathe o'er my dying brain its last monotony.
>
> *Shelley*

But the solitude of the sanctified, the loneliness of the child of God, brings again the glimmering of his Father's feet among the sorrows and the haunts of human beings. And to the broken in heart, to the bound in hereditary prisons, and to the wounded and weak, Jesus our Savior draws near.

> Then on our utter weakness and the hush
> Of hearts exhausted that can ache no more,
> On such abeyance of self and swoon of soul
> The Spirit hath lighted oft, and let men see

That all our vileness alters God no more
Than our dimmed eyes can quench the stars in
　　heaven:—
From years ere years were told, through all the sins,
Unknown sins of innumerable men,
God is himself for ever, and shows to-day
As erst in Eden, the eternal hope.

F. W. H. Myers

Loneliness in Preparation

And Jacob was left alone; and a Man wrestled
with him until the breaking of the day. (Genesis 32:24)

. . . life is not as idle ore,
But iron dug from central gloom,
　　And heated hot with burning fears,
　　And dipt in baths of hissing tears,
And batter'd with the shocks of doom
To shape and use.

Tennyson

It is so human and so like us to be attracted by Jesus, to
be fascinated by His life. But what a sorrowful revulsion
many of us experience when His own words repulse us and
blow out the fires of our emotion; and turning away sorrowful, we leave Jesus alone. Christianity is based on heroism and manifested in martyrdom, and the preparation for
being a Christian is drastic, definite and destructive.

Separation From Possessions
　　Now as He was going out on the road, one came
running, knelt before Him, and asked Him, "Good

Teacher, what shall I do that I may inherit eternal life?" So Jesus said to him, "Why do you call Me good? No one is good but One, that is, God. You know the commandments: 'Do not commit adultery,' 'Do not murder,' 'Do not steal,' 'Do not bear false witness,' 'Do not defraud,' 'Honor your father and your mother.' And he answered and said to Him, "Teacher, all these I have kept from my youth." Then Jesus, looking at him, loved him, and said to him, "One thing you lack: Go your way, sell whatever you have and give to the poor, and you will have treasure in heaven; and come, take up the cross, and follow Me." But he was sad at this word, and went away sorrowful, for he had great possessions. (Mark 10:17–22)

Such was the preparation necessary before this admirable soul could become a disciple of Jesus Christ. To use the language of Dr. Donald Davidson: "Strip yourself of every possession, cut away every affection, disengage yourself from all things, be as if you were a naked soul, alone in the world; be a mere man merely, and then be God's. 'Sell all that you have and follow Me!' Reduce yourself down, if I may say so, till nothing remains but your consciousness of yourself, and then cast the self-consciousness at the feet of God in Christ."

You cannot become a disciple of Jesus Christ rich, a landed proprietor, person of splendid reputation, or with a good name and family. The only road to Jesus is Alone. Will you strip yourself and separate yourself and take that lonely road, or will you, too, go away sorrowful?

"If anyone is in Christ, he is a new creation" (2 Corinthians 5:17). "Do not marvel that I said to you, 'You must be born again' " (John 3:7).

Jesus Christ always speaks from the source of things. Consequently, those who deal only with the surface find Him an offense.

Separation From Professions

Then a certain scribe came and said to Him, "Teacher, I will follow You wherever You go." And Jesus said to him, "Foxes have holes and birds of the air have nests, but the Son of Man has nowhere to lay His head." (Matthew 8:19–20)

Peter said to Him, "Even if all are made to stumble, yet I will not be." And Jesus said to him, "Assuredly, I say to you that today, even this night, before the rooster crows twice, you will deny Me three times." But he spoke the more vehemently, "If I have to die with You, I will not deny You!" And they all said likewise. (Mark 14:29–31)

Professions last as long as the conditions that called them forth last, but no longer. As long as the fervent, strong attachment to Jesus lasts, the professions are the natural expression of that attachment. But when the way grows narrow and reputations are torn, and the popular verdict is against the shameful poverty and meekness of the Son of Man, professions wither on the tongue; not through cowardice, but because the conditions that made the heart warm, and the feelings move and the mouth speak, are altered. When the way of joyfully leaving all and following Jesus in the bounding days of devotion turns into the way of sorrow, and the heroic isolation of being with Jesus ends in shadows, and Jesus seems weak before the world, and the way of following ends in the way of derision, then professions are blighted, and the heart's feelings are frozen or changed into horror and perplexity. Peter's profession ended in denial and disaster: "Then he began to curse and swear, 'I do not know this Man of whom you speak'" (Mark 14:71).

Love never professes; love *confesses.*

From all high and stirring emotions, from all exhilarating professions arising out of true human devotion, our Lord repulses with a stern, bracing rebuke. Sanctified poverty! Ah, it chills the heart and professions die. The poverty of our Lord and His disciples is the exact expression of the nature of the religion of Jesus Christ—just man and God, man possessing nothing, professing nothing; yet when the Lord asks at some dawn, after a heartbreaking failure, "Do you love Me?" the soul confesses, "Yes, Lord; You know that I love You." And when that poverty is a disgust to the full-fed religious world, the disciple does not *profess,* but confesses, with aching hands and bleeding feet, "I love Him," and goes "outside the camp, bearing His reproach."

Professor William James in his pioneer work, *The Varieties of Religious Experience,* says:

> Poverty indeed is the strenuous life—without brass bands, or uniforms, or hysteric popular applause, or lies, or circumlocutions; and when one sees the way in which wealth-getting enters as an ideal into the very bone and marrow of our generation, one wonders whether a revival of the belief that poverty is a religious vocation may not be the transformation of military courage, and the spiritual reform of which our time stands most in need.

We have grown literally afraid of being poor. We despise anyone who elects to be poor in order to simplify and save his inner life. If he does not join the general scramble, and pant with the moneymaking street, we deem him spiritless and lacking in ambition. We have lost the power of imagining what the ancient idealization of poverty could have meant—the liberation from material attachments, the unbribed soul, the manlier indifference, the paying our way by what we are or do, and not by what we have; the right to fling away life at any moment irresponsibly, the more athletic trim, in short, the moral fighting shape.

> For His sake those tears and prayers are offered,
>   Which you bear as flowers to His throne;
> Better still would be the food and shelter,
>   Given for Him, and given to His own.
> Praise with loving deeds is dear and holy,
>   Words of praise will never serve instead;
> Lo! you offer music, hymn and incense,
>   When *He has not where to lay His head.* . . .
> Jesus then and Mary still are with us—
>   Night will find the Child and Mother near,
> Waiting for the shelter we deny them
>   While we tell them that we hold them dear!
>
> A. Procter

Separation From Positions

Then a dispute arose among them as to which of them would be greatest. And Jesus, perceiving the thought of their heart, took a little child and set him by Him, and said to them, "Whoever receives this little child in My name receives Me; and whoever receives Me receives Him who sent Me. For he who is least among you all will be great." (Luke 9:46–48)

"Grant us that we may sit, one on Your right hand and the other on Your left, in Your glory." But Jesus said to them, "You do not know what you ask. Are you able to drink the cup that I drink, and be baptized with the baptism that I am baptized with?" They said to Him, "We are able." So Jesus said to them, "You will indeed drink the cup that I drink, and with the baptism that I am baptized with you will be baptized; but to sit on My right hand and on My left is not Mine to give, but it is for those for whom it is prepared." (Mark 10:37–40)

How we miss it! those loyal, true, human hearts, and ourselves, until we are changed by the deep upheaval of a birth from above, and the presence of an overwhelming love to our Lord in our hearts. The desire to be the "most loyal," the "most faithful," the "holiest" disciple produces a winsome rebuke from our Lord, and our hearts feel we have missed the point but scarcely know how. It was surely natural for the disciples to imagine "which of them would be greatest," and yet when Jesus questioned them, their hearts confused and rebuked them.

"Then Jesus called a little child to Him, and set him in the midst of them, and said, '. . . Therefore whoever humbles himself as this little child is the greatest in the kingdom of heaven' " (Matthew 18:2–4).

By means of the implicit life of a little child Jesus taught the disciples that unless they became "as this little child," they could in no way enter into the kingdom of heaven. The true child of God is such from an inward principle of life from which the life is ordered by implicit loving devotion, as natural as breathing, and as spontaneous as the life of a little child.

"Then another of His disciples said to Him, 'Lord, let me first go and bury my father.' But Jesus said to him, 'Follow Me, and let the dead bury their own dead' " (Matthew 8:21–22).

To plead with Jesus to notice us and enroll us as His disciples from any position—good, bad or indifferent—will meet one of those otherwise unaccountable chills. To seek the lowest position or the highest, or any position at all, is to miss the mark utterly. In the days of preparation from all possessions, professions, and positions, Jesus leads in a separating, isolating way: "What do you seek?" "Whom do you seek?" The sad eyes of the Son of God lure us into the wilderness alone, and these questions ring in our hearts. From all desire for position, place, power, from every pedestal of devotion, or dedication, or deed, He draws and separates us, and suddenly we discern what He wants, deeper than tongue can express. Obedience to the heavenly vision, arising from an abandonment of love to Himself, leads us to heaven. Not as faithful friends, or as moral men, or as devout souls, or as righteous men—Jesus separates us from all these positions by an unbridgeable distance when He is making clear to us that we must leave All. These lonely moments are given to each of us. Have we heeded them?

> Oh, we're sunk enough here, God knows!
>> But not quite so sunk that moments,
> Sure tho' seldom, are denied us,
>> When the spirit' true endowments
> Stand out plainly from its false ones,
>> And apprise it if pursuing
> Or the right way or the wrong way,
>> To its triumph or undoing.

There are flashes struck from midnights,
    There are fire-flames noondays kindle,
Where by piled-up honours perish,
    Where by swollen ambitions dwindle,
While just this or that poor impulse,
    Which for once had play unstifled,
Seems the sole work of a life-time
    That away the rest have trifled.

Browning

Loneliness in Consecration

It is no wonder that preparation has to be so drastic and so deep. It is easy to say things about the necessity of preparation, but we too readily take on the pattern and print of the age, our peers, or the country in which we live. The emphasis today in spiritual domains is on the *work*, not on the *workman*. Three hours is considered sufficient preparation for thirty years' work. But when we turn to the Bible records we almost unconsciously take the deliberate stride of the hills of God, and ever after we have an unhasting and unresting heart amid the cities of humanity. Our Lord Jesus Christ had thirty years' preparation for three years of ostensible work. John the Baptist had a similar preparation, and the apostle Paul spent three lonely years in Arabia. Some words from Dr. Alexander Whyte's individual reading of the apostle Paul will serve to keep us in the right atmosphere for the consideration of this subject of the loneliness in consecration:

> For it was in Arabia, and it was under the Mount of God, that Paul's apostolic ink-horn was first filled with that ink of God with which he long afterwards wrote that so-little-understood writing of his, which we call the seventh of the Romans. A little-understood writing; and no wonder! The apostle

came back from Arabia to Damascus, after three years' absence, absolutely laden down with all manner of doctrines, and directions, and examples for us and for our salvation, if we would only attend to them and receive them. Directions and the examples, of which this is one of the first. That solitude, the most complete and not short solitude, was the one thing that Paul determined to secure for himself immediately after his conversion and his baptism. . . . And thus it is that Holy Scripture is everywhere so full of apartness and aloneness and solitude: of lodges in the wilderness, and of shut doors in the city: of early mornings, and late nights, and lonely night watches: of Sabbath-days and holidays, and all such asylums of spiritual retreat.

Down to Gehenna, and up to the throne,
He travels the fastest who travels alone.

We cannot kindle when we will
        The fire which in the heart resides!
The Spirit bloweth and is still,—
        In mystery our soul abides!
    But tasks in hours of insight willed
    Can be through hours of gloom fulfilled

With aching hands and bleeding feet,
        We dig and heap, lay stone on stone;
We bear the burden and the heat
        Of the long day, and wish 'twere done.
    Not till the hours of light return,
    All we have built do we discern.

Matthew Arnold

The Discipline of Loneliness   165

Consecration is that human action whereby we present ourselves to God. The period of consecration may be three minutes, or thirty years, according to the individual; or the soul may degenerate during its consecration. The period of consecration may be thoroughly misused.

Sanctification begins at regeneration, and goes on to a second great crisis, when God, upon an uttermost abandonment in consecration, bestows His gracious work of entire sanctification. The point of entire sanctification is reached not by the passing of the years but by obedience to the heavenly vision and through spiritual discipline. Spiritual degeneration, so keenly portrayed in the epistle to the Hebrews, is brought about by weak and prolonged consecration, during which the soul degenerates completely.

"Of whom we have much to say, and hard to explain, since you have become dull of hearing. For though by this time you ought to be teachers, you need someone to teach you again the first principles of the oracles of God; and you have come to need milk and not solid food. . . . Therefore, leaving the discussion of the elementary principles of Christ, let us go on to perfection" (Hebrews 5:11–12; 6:1). Perfection here simply means the full maturity of a person's powers; then begins his work.

Separation From Country

Abraham! the "Pilgrim of Eternity," the "Father of the Faithful." These titles give a touch emphatic and decisive to that wonderful career which emphasizes this loneliness in consecration.

> Now the LORD had said to Abram: "Get out of your country, from your kindred and from your father's house, to a land that I will show you" (Genesis 12:1).

By faith Abraham obeyed when he was called to go out to a place which he would receive as an inheritance. And he went out, not knowing where he was going (Hebrews 11:8).

The separation from the ideals and aims and ways of looking at things peculiar to one's social peers, or society, or country, is a great break. To the individual who is undergoing consecration for a supreme sanctification, this separation is a persistent and pressing pain until it is obeyed. To run away from one's country or one's peers is cowardly and un-Christian; that is not Christianity, but cowardly selfishness. One careful glance at our Lord's prayer will kill that cunning cowardice at once: "I do not pray that You should take them out of the world, but that You should keep them from the evil one. They are not of the world, just as I am not of the world" (John 17:15–16).

In Christianity the kingdom and its laws and principles must be put first, and everything else second. If the holy calling demands it, there must be instant and military obedience, leaving all and rallying round the standard of Jesus Christ. The missionary of the Cross is not first a British or an American subject, but a Christian. The missionary is not a sanctified patriot, but one whose sympathies have broken all parochial bounds and whose aims beat in unison with God's own heart.

A Christian is a sanctified man or woman in business, or legal or civic affairs, or artistic and literary affairs. Consecration is not the giving over of the calling in life to God, but the separation from all other callings and the giving over of ourselves to God, letting His providence place us where He will—in business, or law, or science, workshop, politics, or drudgery. We are to be there working according to the laws and principles of the kingdom of God, not according to the ideals or aims or ways of looking at things from the point of view of a particular social group. This constitutes us fools in the eyes of our peers, and the temptation is strong then to get out of our country. It will mean working according to different aims, and we must never take the pattern and print of the social group to which we belong. "Business is business" is not true for the Christian. Business is a sphere of labor in the world where a person exhibits the laws and principles of the kingdom, otherwise he or she is a coward, a deserter, and a traitor to that kingdom. It is a lonely way:

> With a thousand things that are
> Births of woe and food for crime:
> Still, to vindicate the right
> Is a rough and thankless game:—
> Still the leader in the fight
> Is the hindmost in the fame.

Do you answer to the stern, bracing, heroic call in consecration: Get out of your country and stand alone with Jesus? It is a foolish and a shameful thing to be a saint in business. To be a saint may be to be outcast and ridiculed. Try it. Faith is built on heroism. Consecration is the narrow, lonely way to overflowing love. We are not called upon to live long on this planet, but we are called upon to be holy at any and every cost. If obedience costs you your life, then pay it.

> There are few who care to analyze
> The mingled motives, in their complex force,
> Of some apparently quite simple course.
> *One* disentangled skein might well surprise.
> Perhaps a "single heart" is never known,

Save in the yielded life that lives for God alone,—
And that is therefore doubted as a dream
By those who know not the tremendous power
Of all-constraining love!

F. R. Havergal

Separation From Comrades

If anyone comes to Me and does not hate his father and mother, wife and children, brothers and sisters, yes, and his own life also, he cannot be My disciple. (Luke 14:26)

You cannot consecrate yourself *and* your friends. If at the altar your heart imagines that loving arms are still around you, and that together, lovers as lovers, and friends as friends, can enter through this mighty gate of supreme sanctification, it is a fond dream, doomed to disillusionment. Alone! Relinquish all! You cannot consecrate your children, your wife, your lover, your friend, your father, your mother, or your own life as yours. You must abandon all and fling yourself on God as a mere conscious being, and unperplexed, seeking you'll find Him. The teaching that presents consecration as giving to God our gifts, our possessions, our comrades, is a profound error. These are all abandoned, and we give up forever *our right to ourselves.* A sanctified soul may be an artist or a musician, but he is not a sanctified artist or musician: he is one who expresses the message of God through a particular medium. As long as the artist or musician imagines he can consecrate his artistic gifts to God, he is deluded. Abandonment of ourselves is the kernel of consecration, not presenting our gifts, but presenting ourselves without reserve.

Our Lord uses stern words; He says it is better to be deformed than damned:

If your hand or your foot causes you to sin, cut it off and cast it from you. It is better for you to enter into life lame or maimed, rather than having two hands or two feet, to be cast into the everlasting fire. And if your eye causes you to sin, pluck it out and cast it from you. It is better for you to enter into life with one eye, rather than having two eyes, to be cast into hell fire. (Matthew 18:8–9)

The foot and the hand and the eye are great and mighty gifts, and also means of livelihood; yet the stern principle of our Lord is clear—It is better to be deformed than damned. The inner experience of some gifted soul, some genius or orator or artist, who has undergone this test of supreme sanctification, might well expound this marvelously profound experience. Oh, the wail of the souls who have failed at the altar and have made their consecration a wilderness experience years long. Their language wrings with pain.

> I descended into the fire of Hell
> And gazed until I burned;
> I came, but how I came I cannot tell,
> My vile heart led me, being its own spell.
> I looked, was marred,—and turned.
> I entered on a heritage of woe,
> And never can return;
> I broke the heart of God's own Son to go,
> I spurned His Spirit that besought me so,
> And entered Hell to burn.
> And marvel ye that I must watch and pray
> While ye are sweet asleep?
> Lest haply from His saving grace I stray,

Enticed by things with which you play!
Sleep on! but I must weep!

The subject of consecration has been purposely dealt with from its deepest meaning in order that its application to all domains might be made clear. Its one note is "Do you not know . . . you are not your own? For you were bought at a price; therefore glorify God in your body" (1 Corinthians 6:19–20). It is the loving hands, the tender hands, that hinder most at the altar; the hands too loving that prevent. It is a lonely way; we cannot take it with comrades.

> Peter began to say to Him, "See, we have left all and followed You." So Jesus answered and said, "Assuredly, I say to you, There is no one who has left house or brothers or sisters or father or mother or wife or children or lands, for My sake and the gospel's, who shall not receive a hundredfold now in this time—houses and brothers and sisters and mothers and children and lands, with persecutions—and in the age to come, eternal life. But many who are first will be last, and the last first." (Mark 10:28–31)

As in the case of separation from country, this separation from comrades is not a cowardly, selfish, immoral breaking away from human ties which God has ordained. It does mean that, if Jesus demands it, nothing must stand in the way; He must be first. Oh, for more of that abandonment of consecration and fire from heaven which would make a mighty army of saints!

Yes, without cheer of sister or of daughter,
Yes, without stay of father or of son,

The Discipline of Loneliness   171

Lone on the land and homeless on the water
Pass I in patience till the work be done.

Yet not in solitude if Christ anear me
Waketh Him workers for the great employ,
Oh not in solitude, if souls that hear me
Catch from my joyance the surprise of joy.

Hearts I have won of sister or of brother
Quick on the earth or hidden in the sod,
Lo every heart awaiteth me, another
Friend in the blameless family of God.

F. W. H. Myers

This hour of solitude and loneliness in consecration is followed by a blessed sanctified socialism, the hidden secret of which is the heart alone in delight with God. Multitudes of men follow whenever a soul has been on the mount with God. If one might dare whisper it, the blighting suffering in lonely consecration is God's imperial way of making what we once had intermittently our eternal possession.

Separation From Comforts

Yet it was well, and Thou hast said in season
As is the Master shall the servant be:
Let me not subtly slide into the treason,
Seeking an honour which they gave not Thee:
Never at even, pillowed on a pleasure,
Sleep with the wings of aspiration furled,
Hide the last mite of the forbidden treasure,
Keep for my joys a world within the world.

F. W. H. Myers

Nevertheless I tell you the truth. It is to your advantage that I go away; for if I do not go away, the Helper will not come to you; but if I depart, I will send Him to you. . . . Therefore you now have sorrow; but I will see you again and your heart will rejoice, and your joy no one will take from you. (John 16:7, 22)

Interior desolations serve a vital purpose in the soul of a Christian. It is expedient that the joys of contact be removed that our idea of the Christian character may not be misplaced. In the early days of spiritual experience we walk more by sight and feelings than by faith. The comforts, the delights, the joys of contact are so exquisite that the very flesh itself tingles with the leadings of the cloudy pillar by day and the fiery pillar by night; but there comes a day when all that ceases. Madame Guyon in her poem entitled "The Dealings of God; or The Divine Love in Bringing the Soul to a State of Absolute Acquiescence," states this separation from comforts—

> How I trembled then and fear'd,
> When my Love had disappear'd!
> "Wilt thou leave me thus?" I cried,
> " 'Whelm'd beneath the rolling tide?"
> Vain attempt to reach His ear!
> Love was gone, and would not hear.
>
> Ah, return and love me still;
> See me subject to Thy will;
> Frown with wrath, or smile with grace,
> Only let me see Thy face!
> Evil I have none to fear;
> All is good, if Thou art near.
>
> Yet He leaves me,—cruel fate!
> Leaves me in my lost estate.

Have I sinn'd? Oh, say wherein.
Tell me, and forgive my sin!
King and Lord whom I adore,
Shall I see Thy face no more?

Be not angry,—I resign
Henceforth all my will to Thine.
I consent that Thou depart,
Though Thine absence breaks my heart.
Go, then, and forever, too;
All is right that Thou wilt do.

This was just what Love intended:
He was now no more offended;
Soon as I became a child,
Love returned to me and smiled.
Never strife shall more betide
'Twixt the Bridegroom and His bride.

It is difficult to put this experience into language without making God's way seem foolish and an occasion for our petulance. The very essence of Christianity is not so much a walk *with* Jesus as a walk *like* His walk, when we have allowed Him to baptize us with the Holy Spirit and fire. As we pointed out in "The Discipline of Suffering," the disaster of sentiments and emotions indulged in for themselves is that these end in the revenge of the lower nature. So here, delight in experiences heralds the approach of a false mysticism, the characteristic of which is an inwardness of experience developing into a private illumination apart from the written Word. Madame Guyon ran perilously near this danger of quietism.

All ecstasies and experiences, all inner voices and revelations and dreams, must be tested by the pure outer light of

Jesus Christ and His Word. By looking to Him we are changed into the same image from glory to glory, when consecration has been made a definite transaction. Sanity in ordinary human life is maintained by a right correspondence with the facts revealed by our Lord Jesus Christ.

These experiences are not recognized at the time, but in looking back from a more mature stage one's heart comments "Amen" to the exposition of the way God has taken us. All false mysticism arises from the fact that teachers insist on an inner experience, which by the simple process of introspection ultimately kills itself. Subjective states must be tested and estimated and regulated by objective standards. This is the only safeguard against the irresponsible crowd of fanatics who live from hand-to-mouth in spiritual experience and get nowhere, and by reason of their own shallowness, end in contemptible disasters. This elementary state of spiritual experience ought to herald the last stage of a protracted consecration. Thank God these isolating, separating forces may be recognized at the moment of regeneration by intuition, and, by a willing transaction, the soul may be borne on to perfection without these distressing wilderness experiences.

To quote Madame Guyon again; she comments thus on her own experience, long after such experiences had ceased:

> To complete my distress, I seemed to be left without God Himself, Who alone could support me in such a distressing state. The misfortune is that people wish to direct God instead of resigning themselves to be directed by Him. They wish to take the lead and to follow in a way of their own selection, instead of submissively and passively following where God sees fit to conduct them. And hence it is that many souls

The Discipline of Loneliness 175

who are called to the enjoyment of God Himself and not merely to the gifts of God, spend all their lives in pursuing and in feeding on little consolations, resting in them as in their place of delights, and making their spiritual life to consist in them.

All this goes to show that the Christian life simply reconstructs the reasoning from the common-sense facts of natural life, preparing the way for that walk in faith that fears nothing because the heart is blazing with the love of God.

If thou wouldst have high God thy soul assure,
That she herself shall as herself endure,
Shall in no alien semblance, thine and wise,
Fulfill her and be young in Paradise,
One way I know; forget, forswear, disdain
Thine own best hopes, thine utmost loss and gain,
Till when at last thou scarce rememberest now
If on the earth be such a man as thou,
Nor hast one thought of self-surrender,—no,
For self is none remaining to forgo,—
If ever, then shall strong persuasion fall
That in thy giving thou hast gained thine all,
Given the poor present, gained the boundless scope,
And kept thee virgin for the further hope.

F. W. H. Myers

An aside: Possibly the lack of recognizing the human option in this loneliness in consecration has led teachers to blunder unconsciously into a line of teaching perilously dangerous to Christianity. There is in our midst today a strong revival of pagan spirituality. Many are using the terms of Hinduism or of Buddhism to expound Christianity, and they end not in expounding Christianity at all, but in expounding the very human experience of consecration, which is not peculiar to Christianity.

The peculiar doctrine or gospel of the Christian religion is entire sanctification, whereby God takes the most unpromising individual and makes a saint of him or her. The teaching called "Deeper Death to Self" is a misleading form of this doctrine. The sentiments it expresses are so languid and painful, so injurious, that during the stage of consecration there is a sympathetic agreement with the introspective morbid condition that results. Our Lord does not teach a consecrated anemia, that is, the destruction of personality; He teaches a very positive *death forever to my right to myself,* a positive destruction of the disposition of sin and a positive placing in, in entire sanctification, of the Holy Spirit, a pronounced identity that bears a strong family likeness to Jesus. Not "Deeper Death to Self," that is sanctified suicide, but the realization of another's self in love, that other self being God. Jesus Christ emancipates the personality and makes the individuality pronounced. The transfiguring, incalculable element is love, personal, passionate devotion to Himself, and to others. "Deeper Death to Self" is complacent, and enervatingly encouraging to the morbid soul, who having missed the first period of discipleship in consecration, is ever fainting on the *Via Dolorosa,* but never getting to the place where the "old man," *my right to myself,* dies right out. Entire sanctification puts a person's breast and back as either should be, places his feet on earth and his head in heaven, and gives him the royal insignia of the saints.

Loneliness in Sanctification

Then they all forsook Him and fled. Now a certain young man followed Him, having a linen cloth thrown around his naked body. And the young men laid hold of him, and he left the linen cloth and fled from them naked. (Mark 14:50–52)

Stripped for flight or following?

Say, could aught else content thee? which were best,
After so brief a battle an endless rest,
Or the ancient conflict rather to renew,
By the old deeds strengthened mightier deeds to do,
Till all thou art, nay, all thou hast dreamed to be
Proves thy mere root or embryon germ of thee;—
Wherefrom thy great life passionately springs,
Rocked by strange blasts and stormy tempestings,
Yet still from shock and storm more steadfast grown,
More one with other souls, yet more thine own?—
Nay, thro' those sufferings called and chosen then
A very Demiurge of unborn men,—
A very Saviour, bending half divine
To souls who feel such woes as once were thine;—
For these perchance, some utmost fear to brave
Teach with thy truth, and with thy sorrows save.

F. W. H. Myers

The loneliness of preparation and of consecration are more or less complicated by enfeebling intermingling of sin and sympathy and selfishness. Now we come to the loneliness of the serene uplands where the silences of God's eternities are ever around. Oh, it is a great thing when our Father can safely leave us alone on the mountains of God, even if the darkness is unspeakable. The loneliness of a blessed personal responsibility gladly accepted—master of everything, the lover and friend of God. God takes us mighty ways; He takes us by the lonely ways of apprentice-ship, workmanship, and mastership.

Separation In Sifting

> Immediately the Spirit drove Him into the wilderness. And He was there in the wilderness forty days, tempted by Satan, and was with the wild beasts; and the angels ministered to Him. (Mark 1:12-13)

After the baptism by the Holy Spirit and fire, we emerge as masters in the sense of fitness for the work of saints. Then God shows us His greatest mercy, for He spares us no requirement of that mastership, or saint-ship. We find our-selves alone with forces which are working to sift and disin-tegrate, to discourage and destroy; but our inward implicit communion makes us feel the confidence of God in us. It is as if God, smiling, were saying to Satan—"Do your worst; I know that He who is in him is greater than he who is against him." I can recall seeing a picture in the Royal Academy some years ago. It was a picture of lesser impor-tance, but the artist had grasped the lofty loneliness of temp-tation as portrayed in Mark 1:12-13. The wilderness was under a gray, lowering aspect, distance and dreariness and dread was stamped on every rock and stone, and in the midst the figure of Christ stood, alone. No devil or angel was portrayed, only a few prowling wild beasts, accentuat-ing the wild loneliness of that supreme moment of Satanic sifting. Is that same kind of sifting given to us? Surely it is. "For we do not have a High Priest who cannot sympathize with our weaknesses, but was in all points tempted as we are, yet without sin" (Hebrews 4:15).

When our apprenticeship is ended, we are tested as our Lord and Master was. On the threshold of our mastership—or to put it in theological terms, after regeneration and entire consecration, when we have passed the mighty crisis of the baptism of the Holy Spirit and begin our walk, work, and worship under a supreme sanctification, then we are tempted as He was. It is not our object to consider the nature of that temptation, but merely to mention its place and its loneliness. It is not the loneliness of birth pains or growing pains, it is the loneliness of the saint. As in nature so in grace. The first period of our natural lives is one of promise, vision and enthusiasm, in which the surrounding mysteries have a fascination that alternates with fears. Then there comes a time when it is—

> Never again the boy-life,
> Only the pain and joy life—
> More the first than the last.
>
> F. R. Havergal

and all subsequent life holds out the proving of our powers. Saint-ship means mastership. The order of the saintly life is—a witness, a leader, and a commander.

The loneliness of sifting lays the conviction broad and deep that the saint has substituted the will of God for his individual will. The first ordeal of temptation that tries the stuff of which the saint is made is that of loneliness, and it comes on the very threshold of the superconquering life.

> What, if He hath decreed that I shall first
> Be try'd in humble state and things adverse,
> By tribulations, injuries, insults,
> Contempts, and scorns, and snares, and violence,—

Suffering, abstaining, quietly expecting,
Without distrust or doubt,—that He may know,
What I can suffer, how obey?

Milton

Separation in Suffering*

These things I have spoken to you, that in Me you may have peace. In the world you will have tribulation; but be of good cheer, I have overcome the world. (John 16:33)

Men as men,
Can reach no higher than the Son of God,
The Perfect Head and Pattern of mankind.
The time is short and this sufficeth us
To live and die by; and in Him again
We see the same first, starry attribute,
"Perfect through suffering," our salvation's seal
Set in the front of His humanity.

And while we suffer, let us set our souls
To suffer perfectly: since this alone,
The suffering, which is this world's special grace,
May here be perfected and left behind.

H. Hamilton King

The most fundamental thing that can be said about the suffering of the supremely sanctified is that it springs from an active, unquestioning submission to the will of God, allowing God to work out in the life His idea of what a saint should be, just as He worked out in the life of Jesus

---

*This subject is dealt with more fully in "The Discipline of Suffering."

Christ, not what a saint should be, but what a Savior should be. After all that can be said is said, the sufferings of the saint arise not from inbred sin, but from obedience to the will of God which can rarely be stated explicitly. The will of God is apprehended by the Holy Spirit indwelling the saint; it is apprehended not as the mind apprehends a truth, but in the way any incalculable element is intuitively grasped. Inestimable damage is done when the will of God is made an external law to be obeyed by conscious grasp. The will of God is apprehended by an almost unconscious impelling of the indwelling Holy Spirit. It is essentially a lonely way, for the saint knows not why he suffers as he does, yet he comprehends with a knowledge that passeth knowledge that all is well. His language is that of Job: "He knows the way that I take; when He has tested me, I shall come forth as gold" (Job 23:10).

When we understand that the saints are the rich glory of Jesus Christ's inheritance, we have added light on the mystery of the suffering of the saints.

". . . that you may know . . . what are the riches of the glory of His inheritance in the saints" (Ephesians 1:18).

". . . when He comes, . . . to be glorified in His saints and to be admired among all those who believe." (2 Thessalonians 1:10).

The suffering of the saints at heart is not what is ensnaringly known as "Deeper Death to Self." It springs from an active submission and determination to accept the intensely individual responsibility of doing God's will. It is not absorption by loss of individuality; that destroys all possibility of suffering, and indicates the paganizing of the sanctified life so prevalent today. It is rather the transfiguration of individuality in the mastership of God's purpose in Christ. "Till we all come to the unity of the faith and of the knowledge of the Son of God, to a perfect man, to the measure of the stature of the fullness of Christ" (Ephesians 4:13).

The moment in which one enters into the experience of supreme sanctification is the crisis that marks his evangelical perfection. All alien things that retarded and deformed him have been removed. Then begins his life as a master Christian and there is no other kind of Christian on this road. In this supreme sanctification he develops and attains height after height. How clearly the apostle Paul puts these two perfections:

> Not that I have already attained, or am already perfected; but I press on, that I may lay hold of that for which Christ Jesus has also laid hold of me. Brethren, I do not count myself to have apprehended; but one thing I do, forgetting those things which are behind and reaching forward to those things which are ahead, I press toward the goal for the prize of the upward call of God in Christ Jesus. Therefore let us, as many as are mature, have this mind; and if in anything you think otherwise, God will reveal even this to you. Nevertheless, to the degree that we have already attained, let us walk by the same rule. (Philippians 3:12–16)

> And I smiled as one never smiles but once,
> Then first discovering my own aim's extent,
> Which sought to comprehend the works of God,
> And God himself and all God's intercourse
> With the human mind; I understood, no less,
> My fellows' studies, whose true worth I saw,
> But smiled not, well aware who stood by me.

And softer came the voice—"There is a way:
'Tis hard for flesh to tread therein, imbued
With frailty—hopeless, if indulgence first
Have ripened inborn germs of sin to strength:
Wilt thou adventure for my sake and man's,
Apart from all reward?" And last it breathed—
"Be happy, my good soldier; I am by thee,
Be sure, even to the end!"—I answered not,
Knowing him. As he spoke, I was endued
With comprehension and a steadfast will;
And when he ceased, my brow was sealed his own.
If there took place no special change in me,
How comes it all things wore a different hue
Thenceforward?—pregnant with vast consequence,
Teeming with grand result, loaded with fate?
So that when, quailing at the mighty range
Of secret truths which yearn for birth, I haste
To contemplate undazzled some one truth,
Its bearing and effects alone—at once
What was a speck expands into a star,
Asking a life to pass exploring thus,
Till I near craze. I go to prove my soul!
I see my way as birds their trackless way.
I shall arrive! what time, what circuit first,
I—ask not: but unless God send his hail
Or blinding fire-balls, sleet or stifling snow,
In some time, his good time, I shall arrive:
He guides me and the bird. In his good time!

Browning

Separation In Service

Hark, hark! a voice amid the quiet intense!
It is thy Duty waiting thee without—

Rise from thy knees in hope, the half of doubt—
A band doth pull thee—It is Providence!
Open thy door straightway and get thee hence;
Go forth into the tumult and the shout!
Work! love! with workers, lovers all about!
Of noise alone is born the inward sense
Of silence; and from Action springs alone
The inward knowledge of true love and faith.

George MacDonald

Work may be executed by driven slaves or by master workers. A saint is not an instrument of God—he or she is a master worker for God. A person may be used as an instrument of God without being a servant of God; there is no trace of the master workman about him. We, too, may have found that during the days of our apprenticeship God has allowed us to do work, not for Him, but for our own perfecting. But now God takes the saints with skilled finger, so to speak, and with tried and tested patience, into His enterprises to battle and to build. After His resurrection Jesus said to the disciples, "As the Father has sent Me, I also send you" (John 20:21). And again, "Go therefore and make disciples of all the nations" (Matthew 28:19). And in His High Priestly Prayer our Lord prayed: "As You sent Me into the world, I also have sent them into the world" (John 17:18). And the apostle Paul in writing to Timothy said: "Be diligent to present yourself approved to God, a worker who does not need to be ashamed, rightly dividing the word of truth" (2 Timothy 2:15).

All these words breathe activity, energy, and triumphant masterwork. Jesus did not say, "Go and discourse about making disciples," but "Go and *make* disciples." The making of converts is a satanic perversion of this strenuous workmanlike product. How many make followers of their own convictions, and how few make disciples! The production of saints, that is the work. God almighty regenerates people's souls; we make disciples. Are we doing it?

God is apparently not very careful whom He uses or what He uses for the work of regeneration; but none but the master workmen, that is, the saints, can make disciples. Does your work for God stamp the hearts of the people round about you with an enervating, sentimental love for you? or does every remembrance of you cause a strenuous stirring of hearts to do better, grander work for God? God's curse is on the spiritual nature that cannot reproduce its own kind. The apostle Paul cries out exultingly: "For what is our hope, or joy, or crown of rejoicing? Is it not even you in the presence of our Lord Jesus Christ at His coming? For you are our glory and joy" (1 Thessalonians 2:19–20). Can you catch sight of the product? The making of saints. What are you doing with the thousands of souls that God's mighty Spirit is regenerating? Are you stripped and at work, studying, praying, suffering, to make disciples of them?

> Get leave to work
> In this world!—'tis the best you get at all!
> For God in cursing, gives us better gifts
> Than men in benediction. God says *Sweat*
> For foreheads,—men say *Crowns,*—and so we are
>   crowned
> Ay, gashed—by some tormenting circle of steel
> Which snaps with a secret spring.—Get Work! Get
>   Work!
> Be sure 'tis better than what you work to get!
> *Elizabeth Barret Browning*

"Do you love Me? . . . Tend My sheep." Can you feed the lambs and the sheep? Do you, or are you in show business? Listen to the voice of your Master: "As the Father has sent Me, I also send you" (John 20:21). Is it not time for you to present yourself before God and say, "Father, look at my hands, my heart, and my head: Jesus has cleansed me"? And He will answer, "Son, go work today in my vineyard" (Matthew 21:28).

> I too could now say to myself: Be no longer a chaos, but a world, or even 'worldkin.' Produce! Produce! Were it but the most pitiful, infinitesimal fraction of a product, produce it in God's name! 'Tis the utmost that thou hast in thee: out with it then. Up, Up! Whatsoever thy hand findeth to do, do it with thy whole might. Work while it is called today, for the night cometh, wherein no man can work.
>
> *Carlyle*

This loneliness in service is so subtle that if we try and state it in words we almost lose it. It is so easy to coarsen this sublime theme by a word misunderstood, so difficult to put it in any language saving when the heart is in profoundest communion with God. We are so apt to consider work as something done by an individual and yet separate from him or her. The essential peculiarity of the work of the sanctified servant of God is that he never can be separated from his work without a violent outrage.

We are ever apt to overestimate the aloneness of our Lord prefigured by the types and symbols of the old dispensation: the scapegoat, the lamb, and the shed blood; and we ignore that the true prototype of our Lord is the prophet. How continually the prophets break out with some arresting statement that seems fit only in the mouth of our Lord! How often the psalmist bursts out with utterances of an unaccountable touch, the full meaning of which is found for us in Jesus Christ alone. These prophets, these workmen of God, foreshadowed Jesus Christ in their measure, and experienced the awful loneliness of a servant of God. Their desolation sprang from no illusion of weakness, nor from any horror-stricken doubt of God, any more than did the profound cry of our Lord: "My God, My God, why have You forsaken Me?" We discern in the personal, passionate pain of the prophets the true outlines of the workman of God. The character of the prophet is essential to his work. In all other work the character of the workman is made subservient to his skill.

"The Spirit of the Lord came upon Gideon . . ." (Judges 6:34). Before the Holy Spirit can materialize in the saints of this present age as He did in the prophets of old, a perfect holiness, physical, moral and spiritual, is necessary. This is what Jesus Christ has wrought for us in the atonement, and this is what is meant by entire sanctification. On that foundation the true elements of prophecy are built. A prophet is not a sanctified gypsy telling fortunes, but is a person who speaks as he is moved by the Holy Spirit within.

To make disciples, then, we must have been made disciples ourselves. There is no royal road to sainthood and discipleship. The way of the cross is the only way. We see God only from a pure heart, never from an able intellect. The elements in the lot of a workman for God are those that first of all make him a workman, and then constitute him a toiler for God, The workman for God in all probability will have to go the way his Lord and Master went. The first flush of the career of a workman for God may be in glory and acclaim, leading to blessed transfiguration. Then there comes the descent into the valley, deeper and deeper, until in that lonely place, toiling unseen, unknown, unmarked, he reaches in the spirit of travail that sublime agony of loneliness when "Father" seems frozen in his heart, and he cries out, "Why have You forsaken me?" It is not a cry of weakness, nor of imperfection; it is not a cry of doubt in God; it is a cry from the last touch of heroism on the workman for God who is being made conformable to the death of Jesus, not for his own sake or his own perfecting, but for the work of God. It takes him to the threshold of that awful abyss of the master workman Himself, where He was left alone with death and became as lonely as sin. Amid the spiritual ramifications of that unshared, unfathomed experience, He cried out, "My God, My God, why have You forsaken Me?" The workman for God dare not talk, he dare not speculate; but in wonder, love, and awe he thanks God for "the glory and the passion of this midnight," because it has brought him to the threshold of an understanding of the loneliness of Jesus Christ who was made "to be sin for us, that we might become the righteousness of God in Him" (2 Corinthians 5:21).

> And that most closely we may follow Him,
> By suffering, have all hearts of men allowed.
> Is suffering then more near and dear to God
> For its own sake than joy is? God forbid!
> We know not its beginning nor its end;
> Is it a sacrifice? a test? a school? . . . .
> We suffer. Why we suffer,—that is hid
> With Gods foreknowledge in the clouds
>   of Heaven.
>
> *H. Hamilton King*

Dismiss me not Thy service, Lord,
    But train me for Thy will;
For even I in fields so broad
    Some duties may fulfill;
And I will ask for no reward.
    Except to serve Thee still.

Our Master all the work hath done,
    He asks of us to-day;
Sharing His service, every one
    Share too His sonship may:
Lord, I would serve and be a son;
    Dismiss me not, I pray.

T. T. Lynch

Alone With God

Still, still with Thee, when purple morning breaketh,
    When the bird waketh, and the shadows flee;
Fairer than morning, lovelier than daylight,
    Dawns the sweet consciousness, I am with Thee.

Alone with Thee, amid the mystic shadows,
    The solemn hush of nature newly born;
Alone with Thee, in breathless adoration,
    In the calm dews and freshness of the morn.

Harriet Beecher Stowe

There's not a craving in the mind
    Thou dost not meet and still;
There's not a wish the heart can have
    Which Thou dost not fulfill.

All things that have been, all that are,
　　All things that can be dreamed,
All possible creations made,
　　Kept faithful, or redeemed,—

All these may draw upon Thy power,
　　Thy mercy may command,
And still outflows Thy silent sea,
　　Immutable and grand.

O little heart of mine, shall pain
　　Or sorrow make thee moan,
When all this God is all for thee,
　　A Father all thine own?

Faber

"In Your presence is fullness of joy; at Your right hand are pleasures forevermore" (Psalm 16:11). This walk alone with God is an incommunicable rapture that leads more and more through eternal pleasure, eternal prosperity, and eternal paradise.

Eternal Pleasure

"Therefore, behold, I will allure her, will bring her into the wilderness, and speak comfort to her. I will give her her vineyards from there, and the Valley of Achor as a door of hope; she shall sing there, as in the days of her youth, as in the day when she came up from the land of Egypt. And it shall be, in that day," says the Lord, "that you will call Me 'My husband,' and no longer call Me 'My Master'. . . . I will betroth you to Me for ever; yes, I will betroth you to Me in righteousness and justice, in loving-kindness and mercy; I will betroth you to Me in faithfulness, and you shall know the Lord." (Hosea 2:14–16, 19–20)

All that we know of bliss and pleasure in other domains of friendship and fellowship with kindred minds is but the faintest foreshadowing of the unspeakable pleasure of this communion with God alone. How unhesitatingly the language of Scripture mentions human relationships as the only means of suggesting the unspeakable pleasure of this eternal fellowship with God. Just as the language of lovers is inexplicable to an unloving nature, so the language of the heart in its aloneness with God is inexplicable to those not in a like relationship. There are things "not lawful for a man to utter," not because they transcend language, but because they are based on the sacred intimacy of an individual soul united to God in love. It is perilously possible to take the language of love and degrade it into a language that grovels; and it is perilously possible to take the language of the soul alone in these walks of eternal pleasure and degrade it into a wallowing horror.

The daring sufficiency of The Song of Solomon is an example of how easy it is to make that sublime song grovel in Eastern voluptuousness and sensual wallowing. But for the soul walking alone with God its language is the choicest in the whole Bible to adequately express the eternal pleasure of this blessed loneliness:

"Let him kiss me with the kisses of his mouth—for your love is better than wine . . . Your name is ointment poured forth; therefore the virgins love you. Draw me away! We will run after you. The king has brought me into his chambers. We will be glad and rejoice in you. We will remember your love more than wine. Rightly do they love you" (Song of Solomon

1:2–4). Possibly only when we stand alone with God are we in a fit condition to understand the strong words of Jesus and not abuse them: "Do not give what is holy to the dogs; nor cast your pearls before swine, lest they trample them under their feet, and turn and tear you in pieces" (Matthew 7:6).

"This is eternal life, that they may know You, the only true God, and Jesus Christ whom You have sent" (John 17:3). This constitutes eternal life—an increasing knowledge of the unfathomable God and His only begotten Son. This is eternal pleasure—to know Him! How far removed it is from our concept of rewards and crowns and heaven. The way of a soul walking alone with God, unless we know this same unspeakable fellowship, seems a way overshadowed with sadness and insane with fanaticism.

> I stand upon the mount of God,
>   With sunlight in my soul;
> I hear the storms in vales beneath,
>   I hear the thunder's roll.
>
> But I am calm with Thee, my God,
>   Beneath these glorious skies;
> And to the height on which I stand
>   Nor storms nor cloud can rise.
>
> Oh! this is life! oh, this is joy!
>   My God to find Thee so;
> Thy face to see, Thy voice to hear,
>   And all Thy love to know!
>
>   C. B. Bubier

Eternal Prosperity

The eternal God is your refuge, and underneath are the everlasting arms; He will thrust out the enemy from before you, and will say, 'Destroy!' Then Israel shall dwell in safety, the fountain of Jacob alone, in a land of grain and new wine; his heavens shall also drop dew. Happy are you, O Israel! Who is like you, a people saved by the Lord, the shield of your help and the sword of your majesty! Your enemies shall submit to you, and you shall tread down their high places. (Deuteronomy 33:27–29)

A person's idea of prosperity is according to where his hopes are founded—on God or on a hearsay God; on the living God, or on ideas of God. It is in the way alone with God that the soul says with Job: "I have heard of You by the hearing of the ear, but now my eye sees You. Therefore I abhor myself, and repent in dust and ashes" (Job 42:5–6).

Alone with God! It is there that what is hid with God is made known—God's ideals, God's hopes, God's doings. The intense individual responsibility of walking among people, from the standpoint of being alone with the real God, is never guessed until we do stand alone with God. It is a hidden thing, so hidden that it seems not only untenable but a wild, quixotic thing to do, and so it would be if God were not known to be real. This idea is put in refreshing language by Dr. Josiah Strong:

> The supreme need of the world is a real God; not the Great Perhaps, but the great "I am"; not a God of yesterday; not an "absentee" God, but one who is precisely here, not a Sunday God, but an everyday God. . . . Vital religion always realizes God, while irreligion or worldliness is a practical denial of Him; it is living as if God were not; it is leaving out of account the greatest fact in the universe, which is of course the greatest blunder in the universe.

"Esteeming the reproach of Christ greater riches than the treasures in Egypt; for he looked to the reward . . . he endured as seeing Him who is invisible" (Hebrews 11:26–27).

Alone with God! All hope and all aspiration springs from that source, and consequently all prosperity is measured from that source, and prosperity that springs from any other source is looked upon as disastrous. "The pleasure of the Lord" prospered in the hand of His Son, our Lord Jesus Christ, but the disastrous way of failure, as the world measures prosperity. "Yet it pleased the LORD to bruise Him; He has put Him to grief. When You make His soul an offering for sin, He shall see His seed, He shall prolong His days, and the pleasure of the Lord shall prosper in His hand" (Isaiah 53:10).

Going alone with God, the pleasure of Jehovah prospering in our hands! What a pleasure, and what a prosperity! Our Lord walked alone with God; He despised the shame and the bruising, because His Father was working out His good pleasure in His own inscrutable way; and now we follow in His steps, and the pleasure of the Lord shall prosper in our hands.

What is that pleasure? Making disciples. The pleasure of the Lord that prospered in our Lord and Savior was seeing His seed, that is, all that we understand by regeneration and entire sanctification. The pleasure of the Lord God is seen as we walk alone with God while we live and move and have our being in this world. Unstamped by the pattern and print of the age in which we live, we present so many puzzling features that people are obliged to pause and question, and thus the pleasure of the Lord prospers in our hands.

It is a prosperity that, beginning in the innermost of the innermost, works out to the outermost. It is a prosperity which transfigures with the beauty of holiness, a prosperity which, as sure as it is inward, will manifest itself to the utmost limit outwardly.

> He fixed thee 'mid this dance
> Of plastic circumstance,
> This Present, thou, forsooth, wouldst fain arrest:
> Machinery just meant
> To give thy soul its bent,
> Try thee and turn thee forth, sufficiently impressed.

> Look not thou down but up!
> To uses of a cup,
> The festal board, lamp's flash and trumpet's peal,
> The new wine's foaming flow,
> The Master's lips a-glow!
> Thou, heaven's consummate cup, what need'st thou
> with earth's wheel?

> But I need, now as then,
> Thee, God, who mouldest men;
> And since, not even while the whirl was worst,
> Did I,—to the wheel of life
> With shapes and colors rife,
> Bound dizzily,—mistake my end, to slake Thy thirst:

> So, take and use Thy work:
> Amend what flaws may lurk,
> What strain o' the stuff, what warpings past the aim!
> My times be in Thy hand!
> Perfect the cup as planned!
> Let age approve of youth, and death complete the
> same!

Browning

That they all may be one, as You, Father, are in Me, and I in You; that they also may be one in Us, that the world may believe that You sent Me. And the glory which You gave Me I have given them, that they may be one, just as We are one: I in them, and You in Me; that they may be made perfect in one, and that the world may know that You have sent Me, and have loved them as You have loved Me. Father, I desire that they also whom You gave Me may be with Me where I am, that they may behold My glory which You have given Me; for You loved Me before the foundation of the world. O righteous Father! The world has not known You, but I have known You; and these have known that You sent Me. And I have declared to them Your name, and will declare it, that the love with which You loved Me may be in them, and I in them. (John 17:21–26)

Paradise is a beautiful word, with an emphatic meaning which no other word conveys, namely, spiritual and material.

The city had no need of the sun, or of the moon, to shine in it, for the glory of God illuminated it. The Lamb is its light. And the nations of those who are saved shall walk in its light, and the kings of the earth bring their glory and honor into it. Its gates shall not be shut at all by day (there shall be no night there). And they shall bring the glory and the honor of the nations into it. But there shall by no means enter into it anything that defiles, or causes an abomination or a lie, but only those who are written in the Lamb's Book of Life. (Revelation 21:23–27)

This eternal paradise, entered now by those who walk alone with God, must not be spiritualized by a process of abstractions into a mere inward state of soul. This earth will yet be governed by the saints. "The kingdom of the world is become the kingdom of our Lord and of His Christ." The saints, with a tested, heroic mastership of earth and air and sky, will reign in a very real, concrete paradise. Just as we infer from the tangible material world an unseen spiritual substratum, so there is to be a concrete world which will be but the manifestation of this substratum, whereby we may infer its character. It is "by their fruits" that people's character is known, and also society. From this present order of things we infer an unseen power making for disintegration and destruction, yet in every human heart there lurks an implicit hope of a different order. These hopes ever fade and fail, and the vision tarries so long that hearts grow sick and embittered, and all seems to end in a poet's song, or a lover's passionate extravagance, or a dreamer's dream.

But to the soul alone with God the secret is known and made real, and already a paradise has begun that presages a grander and a greater blessedness than has entered into the human heart to imagine. The kingdom, or paradise, which cannot be seen today by those who have never been alone with God, will one day, at a sudden catastrophic stage, alter the configuration of the globe. "The wilderness and the wasteland shall be glad for them, and the desert shall rejoice and blossom as the rose; it shall blossom abundantly and rejoice, even with joy and singing. . . . They shall see the glory of the Lord, the excellency of our God" (Isaiah 35:1–2).

It is not a flimsy, false dream that springs in the human heart, but a real, visible paradise of God; the hope "springs eternal in the human breast" and will be abundantly satisfied. To spiritualize it into the vague and inane is a sickly, unreal tendency.

Alone with God we have the glory that Jesus had, here and now, the glory of His holiness; and being "transformed into the same image from glory to glory," on and on the saints go to each place of attainment, following the Lamb "wherever He goes."

And wonder of wonders, that is, after all, only the end of the stages in time; but when time shall be no more, and the basal principles of our thoughts will no more be time and space—how can we conceive what it will be like!

"But as it is written: 'Eye has not seen, nor ear heard, nor have entered into the heart of man the things which God has prepared for those who love Him' " (1 Corinthians 2:9).

"Beloved, now we are children of God; and it has not yet been revealed what we shall be, but we know that when He is revealed, we shall be like Him, for we shall see Him as He is" (1 John 3:2).

There's a fancy some lean to and others hate—
    That, when this life is ended, begins
New work for the soul in another state,
    Where it strives and gets weary, loses and wins;
Where the strong and the weak, this world's congeries,
    Repeat in large what they practiced in small,
Through life after life in unlimited series;
    Only the scale's to be changed, that's all.
Yet I hardly know. When a soul has seen
    By the means of Evil that Good is best,
And, through earth and its noise, what is heaven's serene,—
    When our faith in the same hath stood the test—
Why, the child grown man, you burn the rod,
    The uses of labor are surely done;
There remaineth a rest for the people of God:
    And I have had troubles enough, for one.

Browning

6

The Discipline of Patience

Wait on the Lord. (Psalm 27:14)

The subject of patience is so largely dealt with in the Bible that it ought to have a much larger place in our Bible studies and talks.

Patience, to most minds, is associated with exhaustion, or with "patients"; consequently anything robust and vigorous seems naturally to connect itself with all that is impatient and impetuous. Patience is the result of well-centered strength. To "wait on the Lord," and to "rest in the Lord," is an indication of a healthy, holy faith, while impatience is an indication of an unhealthy, unholy unbelief. This well-centered strength, or patience, forms a prominent characteristic in the biblical revelation of God, of our Lord Jesus Christ, and of the saints.

> Then on our utter weakness and the hush
> Of hearts exhausted that can ache no more,
> On such abeyance of self and swoon of soul
> The Spirit hath lighted oft, and let men see
> That all our vileness alters God no more
> Than our dimmed eyes can quench the stars in heaven:
> From years ere years were told, through all the sins,

Unknown sins of innumerable men,
God is Himself for ever, and shows to-day
As erst in Eden, the eternal hope.

The Patience of God

> Have you not known? Have you not heard? The
> everlasting God, the LORD, the Creator of the ends of
> the earth, neither faints nor is weary. (Isaiah 40:28)

> Now may the God of patience . . . (Romans 15:5)

How unmoved by, while yet unremoved from, the affairs
of humanity is our God! He changes not and yet He does
not reign in remote regions away from people; He is in the
thick of all their perplexities and loves. The gods of other
religions are unmoved by people's troubles simply because
they do not care; but our God in His love and compassion
imposes on Himself our weakness and pain, while yet He is
unmoved from the well-centered strength of His mighty purposes. If we trace in the Bible with reverence the lines along
which the patience of God most obviously runs, it will well
enrich us. Let us trace, for instance, the patience of God
with:

The World's Ages

According to the Bible, the history of the world is
divided into ages: (1) the pre-Adamic; (2) the Eden; (3) the
Antediluvian; (4) the Mosaic; (5) the Church; (6) the
Kingdom. The remarkable thing in the record of the ages
that have been, and that are, and that are going to be, is that
each age ends in apparent disaster. In this connection read
carefully (1) Genesis 1:2; (2) Genesis 3:24; (3) Genesis 7:19;

(4) John 19:15—16; (5) 2 Thessalonians 2:1—4; (6) Revelation 20:7—9. This is very unexpected for one would naturally suppose that the Bible would show how successful God had been with the world's ages. Successful, that is, in the way we count success; because the Bible does not prove this, people's minds revolt and they say that all God's plans have been overthrown by the devil and God has been checkmated, so to speak. Or else they say that the biblical view is simply the fancy of a few oriental religious men of genius and is not of any use to us nowadays.

Perhaps the illustration of an artist at work on a great canvas will throw more light on the attitude of the God of the Bible to the world's ages. In the preliminary stages of his work the artist may sketch in charcoal and for days execute sketches of varying excellence, and the beauty of these sketches may win our admiration. Then one day we are perplexed to find that he has begun to confuse and obliterate with paints all his beautiful drawings; but he is really interpreting the meaning which was hidden from us.

Or take the old-fashioned way of erecting a scaffolding and building the structure inside. The scaffolding may be so skillfully erected and admirably proportioned and may be there for so long that we come to consider this the scheme in the mind of the architect. Then one day we see the loosening of ropes and planks and ladders, and the turmoil destroys forever the skill and beautiful proportion of the scaffolding; all that is happening is but to clear the real building that it may stand nobly before all as a thing of beauty. There is something similar to the biblical revelation of the way God deals with the world's ages.

There have been prophets and students who handle the Bible like a child's box of bricks; they explain to us the design and structure and purpose, but as time goes on things do not work out in their way at all. They have mistaken the scaffolding for the structure, while all the time God is working out His purpose with a great and undeterred patience.

> The Lord is not slack concerning His promise, as some count slackness, but is longsuffering toward us, not willing that any should perish but that all should come to repentance. (2 Peter 3:9)

To quote again, "There are no dates in His fine leisure." Then we might trace the patience of God with—

The World's Anarchy

> The LORD saw that the wickedness of man was great in the earth . . . . and He was grieved in His heart. (Genesis 6:5–6)

> For He said, "Surely they are My people" . . . . But they rebelled, and grieved His Holy Spirit. . . . (Isaiah 63:8, 10)

Every other view of sin, saving the Bible's view, looks on sin as a disease, a weakness, a blunder, an infirmity; the biblical revelation shows sin to be an anarchy—not a missing of the mark merely, but a refusal to aim at the mark. Sin is that disposition of self-rule which is enmity against God (see Romans 8:7). As one traces from Genesis the clear indication of God's patience with this anarchy, and His working out of the atonement which deals with this fundamental disposition of anarchy against Himself, one realizes the unfathomable, supernatural patience of God. During the ages history proves that sin in the human being makes the heart naturally atheistic. We are all atheists at heart, and the whole world is but a gigantic palace of mirrors wherein we see ourselves reflected, and we call the reflection, God.

"Know that the Lord, He is God; it is He who has made us, and not we ourselves" (Psalm 100:3).

Isaiah 63:8–10, already quoted, exhibits the patience of God with this disposition of anarchy in His own children. In the New Testament this spirit of anarchy is called "the old man," "the carnal mind," which, until it is crucified by identification with the Cross of Christ, will continually rebel and vex His Holy Spirit. It is this spirit of anarchy that has confused the interpretation of God's dealings with people.

Lastly, we might look at the patience of God with:

The World's Acknowledgment

> In returning and rest you shall be saved . . . . But you would not . . . Therefore will the Lord wait, that He may be gracious to you. (Isaiah 30:15, 18)

How longsuffering our God is until we acknowledge Him, and how full of misery and perplexity and sorrow, and worse, people are, until they do acknowledge God.

Erasmus in a wonderful passage shows the unnecessary anguish he went through before he basked in the realization of the acknowledged love of God:

> I must confess it was the very bitterness of extremity that first compelled me to love Him, though of Himself no less lovely than love itself. It was the sharp sauce of affliction that gave edge to mine affections, and sharpened mine appetite to that sweet meat that endureth to everlasting life. But now having had some little foretaste of Him, I am

ever in a holy ecstasy, so ravished, so transported, with a fervent desire of Him and of His presence, that where I am, there am I not; and where I am not, there I am. The soul is where it loveth, not where it dwelleth.

"God demonstrates His own love toward us, in that while we were still sinners, Christ died for us" (Romans 5:8).

The phrase "His own love" is very beautiful; it is God's own peculiar individual love, just as the love of a mother is her own peculiar love, and the love of a father is his own peculiar love. Every different kind of love illustrates some aspect of God's love, but it must not be forgotten that the love of God is His own peculiar love. The word translated *commend* demonstrates conveys the meaning of *recommend*. Because of the disposition arising from anarchy against God, people do not see or believe that the cross of Christ is the expression of God's own love. But when someone is convicted of sin, he begins to discern the marvelously patient love of God, and as he looks at the cross his heart slowly realizes: "Surely now I see—He has borne *my* griefs, and carried *my* sorrows: yet I did esteem Him stricken, smitten of God, and afflicted; but He was wounded for *my* transgressions." Such a moral vision is an acknowledgment of God's own patient love with a twofold verdict: first, that God is love, and second, that the natural human heart is desperately wicked.

Until the world acknowledges God, very often the outcome of the patience of God is that His purposes are carried out in humanity's bad time, and not, as so many say, in God's good time. God's good time is *Now* and His children as well as others cause the repetition of His words in Isaiah 30:15, "In returning and rest you shall be saved; in quiet-

30:15, "In returning and rest you shall be saved; in quiet-ness and in confidence shall be your strength. But you would not." Beware of going to sleep on the decrees of God. In regard to the fulfillment of some of these decrees, such as our salvation and sanctification and sacramental service, it is not a submissive waiting that is required, but the flinging up of our hands and the acknowledgment of God's right to us.

There is one solemn, unwelcome word of warning—do not despise God's patience and keep Him waiting beyond the limit. "Knowing this first: that scoffers will come in the last days, walking according to their own lusts, and saying, 'Where is the promise of His coming? For since the fathers fell asleep, all things continue as they were from the begin-ning of creation'" (2 Peter 3:3–4).

The Patience of Our Lord

> Looking unto Jesus . . . who . . . endured the cross, despising the shame, and has sat down at the right hand of the throne of God. For consider Him . . . lest you become weary and discouraged in your souls. (Hebrews 12:2–3)

In many sections of the Christian community today enthusiasm for humanity is the main characteristic, but it gives a sudden alteration to this point of view when we consider the life of our Lord Jesus Christ, and notice that His first obedience was to the will of His Father, not to the needs of humanity. It is a difficult matter to adjust the rela-tionship of these two callings, but the delicate adjustment is brought about by the Spirit of God. The Spirit and the Word of God ever put first things first, and the first thing is love to God and obedience to God, and the second, service to humanity.

Let us consider the subject of the patience of our Lord under three heads: The Father's Will, the Father's Weakness, and the Father's Waiting.

The Father's Will

The underlying element in Satan's temptation of our Lord is his seeking to remove the "first thing." Satan tempted our Lord as he tempted the first Adam, to do God's work in His own way. The underlying point in the strenuous replies of our Lord is always in one direction—God and God's will first. "I have come down from heaven, not to do My own will, but the will of Him who sent Me" (John 6:38). Hebrews 10:7 emphasizes this: "I said, 'Behold, I have come—in the volume of the book it is written of Me—to do Your will, O God.' " The light thrown on the sufferings of our Lord as an individual will interpret the remarkable statement in Hebrews 5:8: "Though He was a Son, yet He learned obedience by the things which He suffered."

In speaking of our Lord Jesus Christ we must bear in mind that we are dealing with a unique being, of whom it is distinctly said that He "emptied Himself" to marked limitations (see Philippians 2:6–7). This point is mentioned here to show that the sufferings of our Lord did not consist in a willfulness contrary to His Father's will, but in the fact that He, without question, let God the Father express through His life what the Savior of the world should be.

"Father, if it is Your will, take this cup away from Me; nevertheless, not My will, but Yours, be done" (Luke 22:42).

The patience of our Lord with the Father's will and the Father's purpose is a wonderful topic to study, and it explains also the harsh misunderstanding criticisms that have been made during the past centuries.

The next aspect in which the patience of our Lord exhibits itself is more startling, and at the same time more illuminating, namely, the patience of our Lord with:

The Father's Weakness

The phrase, "the weakness of God," is astonishing, but scriptural. "The weakness of God is stronger than men" (1 Corinthians 1:25). Our astonishment arises from the fact that what we call strength from the natural standpoint may be weakness; and that what God calls strength is too often esteemed by people as weakness. It was so in the life of Jesus Christ judged from the standpoint of the natural man. The Father's weakness is exhibited in the aspects of the cradle, the cross, and the called.

In Isaiah 7:14, the word comes: "The Lord Himself will give you a sign: Behold, the virgin shall conceive and bear a Son, and shall call His name Immanuel."

How much attention, think you, could the mighty Roman Empire, the tramp of whose legions shook the world and whose laws girdle it till now, pay to that little babe born of a Jewish peasant girl and laid in a cow's trough! It was beneath the possibility of that gigantic world power's notice. As a prominent modern writer has stated:

> All the empires and the kingdoms have failed, because of this inherent and continual weakness; they were founded by strong men, and upon strong men, but this one thing, the historic Christian Church, was founded upon a weak man, and for that reason it is indestructible, for no chain is stronger than its weakest link.

The writer points out the thing that we are emphasizing, God's ways of working are weakness from the human standpoint.

How patient our Lord ever was with the weakness of God! And He never explains Himself to anyone except as he receives, recognizes and relies on the Holy Spirit. Our Lord could have commanded twelve legions of angels to His assistance, but He did not.

"Do you think that I cannot now pray to My Father, and He will provide Me with more than twelve legions of angels?" (Matthew 26:53).

What weakness! Our Lord lived thirty years in Nazareth with His brothers who did not believe in Him (see John 7:5); He lived three years of popularity, scandal, and hatred; He fascinated a dozen illiterate men who at the end of three years all forsook Him and fled (see Mark 14:50); finally He was taken by the powers that be and crucified outside the city wall. Judged from every standpoint save the standpoint of the Spirit of God, His life was a most manifest expression of weakness, and the idea would be strong to those in the pagan world who thought anything about Him that surely now He and His crazy tale were stamped out.

It is this factor of weakness that alone expounds the revelation given in the Old Testament as well as in the New.

"He shall grow up before Him as a tender plant, and as a root out of dry ground. He has no form nor comeliness; and when we see Him, there is no beauty that we should desire Him" (Isaiah 53:2).

Yet when human wisdom is rendered foolishness by the breaking forth of the Spirit of God, he understands the unspeakable wisdom of God and the unspeakable strength of God to lie in what he before called foolishness and weakness.

'Tis the weakness in strength that I cry for! my flesh,
   that I seek
In the Godhead! I seek and I find it. O Saul, it shall be
A Face like my face that receives thee; a Man like to me,
Thou shalt love and be loved by, for ever! a Hand
   like this hand
Shall throw open the gates of new life to thee! See
   the Christ stand!

What is as weak as one baby? Another! And so our Lord Himself taught that we must all become babes. No wonder Paul says:

"You see your calling, brethren, that not many wise according to the flesh, not many mighty, not many noble, are called" (1 Corinthians 1:26). (See also John 3:7 and Matthew 18:2–3.)

It is the "baby" weakness which is so misunderstood in the New Testament teaching, and the patience of our Lord with us until we learn the absolute necessity of being born from above is only equaled by His own patience with His Father's will.

"God has chosen the foolish things of the world . . . the weak things of the world . . . and the base things of the world, and the things which are despised, . . . and the things which are not" (1 Corinthians 1:27–28).

In every age it has always been the despised crowd that have been called Christians.

The Cross, the climax of our Lord's earthly life, is likewise an exhibition of the weakness of God.

"We preach Christ crucified, to the Jews a stumbling block and to the Greeks foolishness" (1 Corinthians 1:23).

Probably in the Cross more than in any other aspect of our Lord's life do we see the stumbling block presented to the wisdom of the world. Wise men and women of intelligence after the flesh cannot understand why God does not speak. Misunderstanding, prejudices, and unbelief prevail among all until by receiving the Spirit of God as babes they perceive that our Lord Jesus Christ, from the cradle to the Cross, is God's great eternal Word.

Let us look at the final aspect of our Lord's patience:

The Father's Waiting

He must reign till He has put all enemies under His feet. (1 Corinthians 15:25)

It is vastly important to remember that our duty is to fit our doctrines to our Lord Jesus Christ and not to fit our Lord into our doctrines. Our Lord is God-Man, not half God and half human, but a unique being revealed from heaven, and the Holy Spirit alone can expound Him. Let us emphasize again what has been already emphasized, namely, that our Lord Incarnate distinctly subjected Himself to limitations.

"Of that day and hour no one knows, not even the angels in heaven, nor the Son, but only the Father" (Mark 13:32).

Much discussion is thus foreclosed that would otherwise gather round and confuse the life of our Lord and His temptations, insofar as these are disclosed to us.

The patience of our Lord with the Father's waiting is truly a great and wonderful deep. God the Father on occasion witnessed to His Son: "This is My beloved Son . . . . Hear Him" (see 2 Peter 1:17–18); but yet God never vindicated His Son to the people of His own generation because it was not the Father's purpose to do so. He, in silence, left Him on the cross to the supreme satire of the Jews, and our Lord, too, was silent: "He opened not His mouth." Read prayerfully Mark

15:29–32, and note what might be termed the "Dilemma of Golgotha" in which Christ's own words were turned into a cruel jest and hurled back into His face while He was on the cross. The way of sorrow for our Lord was turned into a way of derision. Men laughed while God's heart broke, and thus while hard slanders rose against God and against His Christ, the Father waited. With pure supernatural patience, the prayer arose from the lips of our Lord: "Father, forgive them, for they do not know what they do" (Luke 23:34).

The patience of God and the patience of our Lord is working to one grand divine event, and our Lord knows, as He did in the days of His flesh, how all His saints are straitened till it be accomplished.

"I have a baptism to be baptized with and how distressed I am till it is accomplished!" (Luke 12:50).

> Right for ever on the scaffold,
>   Wrong for ever on the throne;
> But that scaffold sways the future,
>   And behind the dim unknown
> Standeth God within the shadows,
>   Keeping watch upon His own.
>
> *James Russell Lowell*

The Patience of the Saints

> We are bound to thank God always for you, . . . for your patience and faith in all your persecutions and tribulations that you endure. (2 Thessalonians 1:3–4)

The life of faith is the life of a soul who has given over every other life but the life of faith. Faith is not an action of

the mind, nor of the heart, nor of the will, nor of the sentiment, it is the centering of the entire man or woman in God.

The Patience of Faith

The heroes of faith cataloged in the eleventh chapter of
Hebrews were not people who vaguely trusted that some-
how good would be the final goal of ill, they were heroes
who died "in faith" (see verse 13), not faith in a principle,
but faith in a person who promises.

"Since we are surrounded by so great a cloud of witnesses . . . let us run with endurance [patience] the race that
is set before us" (Hebrews 12:1).

This cloud of witnesses is not a noble army of poets, or
dreamers, or thinkers, but a noble army—

> . . . who through faith subdued kingdoms,
> worked righteousness, obtained promises, stopped
> the mouths of lions, quenched the violence of fire,
> escaped the edge of the sword, out of weakness
> were made strong, became valiant in battle, turned
> to flight the armies of the aliens. (Hebrews
> 11:33–34)

These mighty acts were not wrought by diplomacy, but by
faith in God, and we are urged to run with patience this
same way of faith, "looking unto Jesus."

In dealing with the patience of the saints, the subject
naturally unfolds itself into the patience of faith, the
patience of hope, and the patience of love. We have already
indicated the chief matter in the patience of faith, namely,
faith in a person who promises.

"The testing of your faith produces patience. But let
patience have its perfect work, that you may be perfect and
complete, lacking nothing" (James 1:3–4).

"When the Son of Man comes, will He really find faith on the earth?" (Luke 18:8).

"Here is the patience and the faith of the saints" (Revelation 13:10).

"Here is the patience of the saints; here are those who keep the commandments of God and the faith of Jesus" (Revelation 14:12).

These passages assuredly serve to indicate how prominent a place patience plays in God's plans for His saints. It brings again prominently to the front what was stated earlier: that patience is an indication of strong spiritual health, not of weakness and enervation.

The Patience of Hope

> We were saved in this hope. . . . But if we hope for what we do not see, we eagerly wait for it with perseverance [patience]. (Romans 8:24–25)

> Rejoice in hope of the glory of God . . . . knowing that tribulation produces perseverance [patience]; and perseverance, character; and character, hope. Now hope does not disappoint. (Romans 5:2–5)

> Be patient, brethren, until the coming of the Lord . . . . You also be patient. Establish your hearts. (James 5:7–8)

> I, John, both your brother and companion in the tribulation and kingdom and patience of Jesus Christ . . . . (Revelation 1:9)

The faith of the saints is, as it were, a God-given sixth sense which takes hold on the spiritual facts that are revealed in the Bible. The hope of the saint is the expectation and certainty of human nature transfigured by faith. Let it be borne in mind that hope not transfigured by faith dies. "But we were hoping that it was He who was going to redeem Israel" (Luke 24:21). Hope without faith loses itself in vague speculation, but the hope of the saints transfigured by faith grows not faint, but endures "as seeing Him who is invisible."

The saint in the discipline of patience enters into an experimental understanding of the patience of God and the patience of our Lord. The saint has been crucified with Christ and testifies: "It is no longer I who live, but Christ lives in me; and the life which I now live in the flesh I live by faith in the Son of God" (Galatians 2:20).

The saint bears a strong family likeness to his Lord, "weak in Him" (2 Corinthians 13:4). The saint with a glad alacrity can be humiliated or emptied or despised; he or she can also with untainted holiness be exalted or filled or abounding (see Philippians 4:12). The hope of the saint gives the true value to the things seen and temporal. In fact the real enjoyment of things seen and temporal is alone possible to the saint because one sees them in their true relationship to God. The sickening emptiness of the worldly-minded who grasp the things seen and temporal as though they were eternal, is unknown to the saint. The characteristic of the saint is not so much the renunciation of the things seen and temporal as the perfect certainty that these things are but the shows of reality. The patience of hope does not turn men and women into monks and nuns, it gives men and women the right use of this world from another world's standpoint.

"We do not lose heart. . . . while we do not look at the things which are seen, but at the things which are not seen. For the things which are seen are temporary, but the things which are not seen are eternal" (2 Corinthians 4:16, 18).

The Patience of Love

The character produced by the patience of hope is one that exhibits the expulsive power of a new affection.

> Now abide faith, hope, love, these three; but the greatest of these is love. (1 Corinthians 13:13)

> . . . that the love with which You loved Me may be in them. (John 17:26)

> Because you have kept My command to persevere, I also will keep you from the hour of trial. (Revelation 3:10)

There is one sovereign preference in the Bible, namely, love toward God. That love is not a sentiment, but it is the prayerful activity of a perfectly adjusted relationship between God and the saint. Love in the Bible is One; it is unique, and the human element is but one aspect of it. It is a love so mighty, so absorbing, so intense that all the mind is emancipated and entranced by God; all the heart is transfigured by the same devotion; all the soul in its living, working, waking, sleeping moments is indwelled and surrounded in the rest of this love. The saint at times soars like the eagle, he runs like the exuberant athlete, he walks with God and knows no reaction, he faints not nor falters in the largeness of the way (see Mark 12:29–31). Like Tennyson's Sir Galahad, his strength is as the strength of ten, because his heart is pure.

> . . . that you, being rooted and grounded in love, may be able to comprehend with all the saints what is the width and length and depth and height—to

know the love of Christ which passes knowledge; that you may be filled with all the fullness of God (Ephesians 3:17–19).

The patience of love works out in the practical true life of the saint; it is a love that suffers long and is kind. "Love does not envy."

The saint has one striking characteristic, and that is in loving with a divine love—its thirst is not so much to be loved as to be lovable. The characteristics in the life of the saint are the characteristics of our Lord's life. The saint bears a strong family likeness to Jesus Christ.

"My command to persevere [the word of my patience]" is a striking phrase. It cannot be the patience of pessimism because that was not the characteristic of the patience of our Lord; neither is it the patience of exhaustion, for "He shall not fail nor be discouraged." It is surely the patience of love, the patience of joyfulness, which knows that God reigns and rules and rejoices, and that His joy is our strength.

The patience of the saints may be illustrated by the figure of a bow and arrow in the hands of God. He sees the target and takes aim. He strains the bow, not to breaking point, however severe the strain may seem to the saint, but to just that point whence the arrow will fly with surest, swiftest speed to the bull's-eye.

The patience of the saints, like the patience of our Lord, puts the sovereignty of God over all the saint's career, and because the love of God is shed abroad in our hearts by the Holy Spirit, we choose by our free will what God predestines. For the mind of God, the mind of the Holy Spirit, and the mind of the saint are all held together by a oneness of personal, passionate devotion.

Work, for the Day is coming!
    Made for the saints of light;
Off with the garments dreary,
    On with the armour bright:
Soon will the strife be ended,
    Soon all our toils below;
Not to the dark we're tending,
    But to the Day we go.

Work, then, the Day is coming!
    No time for sighing now!
Harps for the hands once drooping,
    Wreaths for the victor's brow,
Now morning Light is breaking,
    Soon will the day appear;
Night shades appall no longer,
    Jesus, our Lord, is near.

Note to the Reader

The publisher invites you to share your response to the message of this book by writing Discovery House Publishers, P.O. Box 3566, Grand Rapids, MI 49501, U.S.A. or by calling 1-800-653-8333. For more information about other Discovery House publications, contact us at the same address and phone number.